A PASSION FOR
PARTIES

A PASSION FOR
PARTIES

Your Guide to
Elegant Entertaining

DAVID TUTERA
AND LAURA MORTON

Simon & Schuster
New York London Toronto Sydney Singapore

Photography Credits

Every effort has been made to contact the photographers whose work is reproduced in this volume.

Ron Aira, page 35; Andre Baranowski, pages 1, 2, 3, 4–5, 6, 7 (except bottom right), 8, 12, 13, 15, 38, 42, 45, 47, 50, 52, 54, 56, 57, 58–59, 61, 62, 63, 64–65, 67 (left and top right), 68, 70, 71, 74, 76, 78, 79, 80, 82, 84, 86–87, 90, 94, 96, 104, 105, 106, 111, 112, 114, 115, 116, 117, 126, 128, 130, 131, 134–135, 136, 137, 139, 140, 141, 144, 145, 146, 150, 151, 152–153, 154, 182, 183; Tom Eckerle, pages 27, 30–31, 85, 89; Nadine Froger, pages 11, 18, 66, 157, 158, 160, 161, 185; Michael Kress, pages 132, 179, 181; Judy Lawne, pages 7 (bottom right), 16, 20, 22–23, 25, 41, 43, 53, 67 (bottom right), 72–73, 91, 101, 102, 107, 109, 118–119, 120, 122, 123, 125, 133, 134 (top), 142, 143, 162–163, 164, 165, 166–167, 168, 169, 170, 172 (left), 172–173, 174, 175, 176, 177; Tom Rollo, page 46.

SIMON & SCHUSTER
Rockefeller Center
1230 Avenue of the Americas
New York, NY 10020

SIMON & SCHUSTER and colophon are registered trademarks of Simon & Schuster, Inc.

For information about special discounts for bulk purchases, please contact Simon & Schuster Special Sales: 1-800-456-6798 or business@simonandschuster.com.

Designed by Joel Avirom
Design Assistants: Jason Snyder and Meghan Day Healey

Manufactured in the United States of America

10 9 8 7 6 5 4 3 2 1

Library of Congress Cataloging-in-Publication Data

Tutera, David, date.
    A passion for parties : your guide to elegant entertaining / David Tutera and Laura Morton.
        p. cm.
    Includes index.
        1. Parties. I. Morton, Laura, date. II. Title.

TX731.T88 2001
642'.4—dc21
                                                        2001032850

ISBN 0-7432-0228-7

To my mom and dad
whose love, encouragement, and guidance
provided me with my passion for life

Contents

Introduction

It's the hottest ticket in town—next to the actual Grammy Awards show, that is. The enormous task I was asked to undertake in planning this event has left me numb with shock and a sense of being totally overwhelmed. It's the Fortieth Annual Grammy Night, an evening filled with excitement and glamour for everyone associated with the music industry. It occurred to me more than once that on this particular night I would be scrutinized by some of the most discerning and hard-to-please people in the world.

The call from the National Academy of Recording Arts and Sciences (NARAS) came six months prior to the event. I was taken aback because for the first time in my career I was being asked to design an event without having to *bid* on it. "This is it!" I thought to myself. "I've finally made it!" Until then I had felt sure my work was special and that I was very good at it, but I had never received any public confirmation.

Many parties are given by various record companies on Grammy night, but I had been asked to plan the granddaddy of them all, the official NARAS party, attended by almost every guest of the show and every record executive in New York that night—some three thousand people. Wow! If anyone had said twelve years previously that I'd have one of the premier event assignments on the planet, I would have laughed and said, "Yeah, sure, that's what I'll be doing," as I drove away in my Volkswagen bus to deliver my next singing telegram dressed as a giant chicken.

I had never planned on being a party producer and event coordinator. My dreams were about becoming a movie star someday or perhaps working in the theater or on Broadway. To support myself in the early years I started a singing telegram company, writing original songs and delivering them dressed as either a giant chicken or a gorilla. (Now you know why singing telegram companies are mostly out of business these days: I ruined it for everyone!) I admit that I cringe a little when remembering those times because some of my current clients are those to whom I delivered those pathetic song-and-dance routines. Thank God I'm the only one who remembers it. But with all the hoopla, I never lost my love for the theater and performing.

Nothing makes a stronger statement at a festive party than a drop-dead gorgeous flower arrangement.

9

As my telegram company began to grow, I received requests for balloon bouquets and other festive gifts. In fact, business was so good that I was able to open a retail store in Larchmont, New York. Then one day a woman came into my store and changed my life forever. She was planning a bar mitzvah for her son and thought it would be wonderful to decorate the party with fabulous arrangements of balloons. Not wanting to spend a fortune on decorating, she thought that balloons were a reasonable compromise. When I agreed to decorate the party, I went from "David the singing chicken and dancing gorilla" to "David the businessman and party planner." It was imperative that I do a really good job for my first client, so I made sure every detail was perfect. In addition, I went to my grandfather, who had owned a very successful floral shop, and asked him if he would train me to carry on his legacy. He taught me everything he knew about floral design and purchasing. The bar mitzvah was a success, and many of those who attended the party called me when they were planning their parties. My business was on its way.

When I outgrew the balloon shop, I opened a larger space next door and began taking on more responsibilities: The party planning business now included designing parties and events. "David the party planner" became "David the event producer." It wasn't long before I was planning every detail of specific events and loving what I was doing. My background in theater assisted me in designing what I thought of as full productions that went from opening night to the closing curtain within a five-hour time span. Much planning and careful rehearsal go into my productions. The lighting is dramatic, the ambience lovely. Every room is carefully thought out and designed to guarantee an enjoyable experience for my clients and their guests. I often tell my clients that we will have succeeded if we can bring a touch of excitement to the guests and shelter them from their cares during the hours of the event. That thought always gets a grin—and usually gets me the job.

A Passion for Parties is a look at the intricacies of event planning, with examples of some of my best work. This book is for your enjoyment, education, and amusement. Having made a career out of planning magical and memorable evenings for hundreds of wonderful clients and thousands of dazzled guests, I consider it an honor to give you a peek inside the fantastic world in which I live every day. My hope is that you enjoy this journey of pomp, pleasure, and passion. After all, life is just a party, isn't it? Well, it should be!

A PASSION FOR
PARTIES

1 | Planning Your Event

As a party planner and event producer, I have the opportunity to work with many different people on a variety of budgets, from excessive to insufficient. Regardless of the cost, though, I always make it work. Occasionally a client thinks I can wave a magic wand and—whammo! presto!—they can have a million-dollar look for virtually nothing. Hey, I may be good, but I'm no David Copperfield.

It's important to understand that spending a lot of money isn't what a great party is all about. Style, taste, and elegance can be achieved at any price—provided you know the right things to do.

The one essential tool to planning any party begins with passion. A great party should indulge every sense: sight, sound, taste, smell, and touch. Keeping those five elements in mind helps you to make a party memorable. If you use this approach for your party, your guests will surely leave delighted and fulfilled.

From the moment guests step into the party space, everything they are connected to should capture the spirit and feeling. What they see, hear, smell, touch, and taste make up the formula for my style of party, but guests should not be aware that their senses are being seduced. They should experience everything as one whole rather than as individual parts. The food shouldn't stand out more than the entertainment, and the lighting shouldn't overshadow the floral

For a casual but elegant dinner party at home, a Tuscan-style table can incorporate fruit, vegetables, and flowers for a rustic beauty. A fresh artichoke cut flush at the base makes a perfect place card holder.

Mr. & Mrs.
Jeremy Smythe

designs. If done properly, each element collectively creates the overall theme and reflects the desired effect of the host or hostess.

My friends often ask me for ideas when they entertain at home, and for the most part they all want the same thing: beauty on a budget—which I prefer to call "affordable elegance." That's what I do best—turn beauty on a budget into affordable elegance. I am an expert at camouflaging the budget (unless it's excessively skimpy) without sacrificing the concept. Most of my clients are sticklers about how their money is spent—and rightfully so. Interestingly, when I entertain in my own home, I never have to spend a lot of money to make a memorable party, and neither do you. Almost all of us will plan an important party or event at some point in our time. To help guide you through the fun but often challenging process of planning such an event, this book offers innovative and unusual ideas to orchestrate an affair to remember. It will fast become the essential guide to planning your own special event and, of equal importance, will help take the stress out of the process.

My sixteen years of experience enable me to guide you through all the elements that make a party great by illustrating different options, ideas, and designs for every occasion. I have planned various types of events, large and small, grand and intimate—including the official Grammy Awards celebration, the opening season gala at the Kennedy Center with Tony Bennett, a fund-raiser hosted by Nancy Reagan honoring His Royal Highness the Prince of Wales, and a birthday party given by Elton John. I have covered every possible scenario in party planning and hosting, from weddings and bar mitzvahs to surprise birthday parties and extravagant backyard barbecues. Whatever your needs are, this book will show you how to turn your fantasy into a happening reality. I have learned the ins and outs of making any event memorable and have faced every circumstance that possibly can challenge even the most experienced party host.

WHAT'S THE OCCASION?

The first thing I ask a new client is "What is the reason you're having a party?" I can then tailor my ideas to the type of party to be held. The options are limitless. I've planned formal weddings for five hundred

people and informal civil ceremonies for ten. I've planned formal dinner parties in great mansions and have entertained eight friends in my backyard. I've coordinated birthday parties for the very young and for the very young at heart—and even parties for no reason at all. (Who says you need to have a reason for throwing a great party, anyway?) Regardless of the occasion, the basic process is pretty much the same. So, step one is simple: Determine the type of party you want to have, such as a wedding, holiday gathering, dinner party, anniversary, cocktail party, casual get-together, or birthday.

A Texas-themed picnic was created using an oversize throw, your basic picnic basket, and bell peppers holding the dipping sauces.

SELECT THE DATE

One of the first decisions you have to make to successfully plan any event is to decide on the date. Everything you plan will depend on that date. Some people plan as far as three years in advance to make sure they can secure their location and all their vendors, such as bands, caterers, decorators, and, of course, party planners. It's really important to look at a calendar when choosing the date. I have very strong feelings about selecting a date for a major event that coincides with a national or religious holiday. Weekends such as Memorial Day, which for most people is considered the first official weekend of the summer, and Labor Day, traditionally the last weekend of the summer, are challenging dates to throw a party. How many times have you been invited to an event on those weekends and simply loathed the idea of having to be somewhere when you'd rather be at the beach or barbecuing at home? I try to dissuade my clients from choosing dates that conflict with holidays because I know that it is a burden for those guests who have other obligations during those times. If possible, try to avoid holiday weekends.

TUTERA TIP: While booking your party for a Friday or Sunday evening may be less expensive at hotels and restaurants, be sure to consider your guests who are traveling a long distance or working late hours.

Attending an event should never be a chore or obligation for guests. It is a time of celebration, and you want to plan your party with that feeling of jubilation.

When selecting the date, consider the weather conditions that might affect the travel needs of out-of-town guests. If you choose to have a winter wedding and you live in an area that is affected by winter

storms, this is definitely a factor to be considered. Many times it is a nonissue, but even the best party planners have no control over Mother Nature, so be aware of the potential pitfalls if you have an event during the winter months. A winter party that is primarily filled with local guests will be far less stressful for you as a host.

When hosting a party at a particular venue, such as a hotel or restaurant, I have found that some days can be less expensive than others. If you take the time to do a comparative analysis, you may find that you can save money by choosing Friday night instead of Saturday or a day event instead of an evening event. Usually a Sunday party is even less expensive, so if you're flexible and cost is a concern, look into your options.

I always recommend having a second and even a third choice of date for the party as a backup. Sometimes a particular location is available on a certain date but the other vendors, such as the band, are not. Coordinating all the key players for one date is not an easy task, so second and third choices of dates are essential.

TOP *For a birthday party at the beach, guests were entertained with games and water sports.*

ABOVE *Beach balls were an inexpensive way to add color to the dining area.*

CHOOSING A LOCATION

Once you've selected a date, deciding on a location is the next step. Depending on the type of party you're hosting, the location must accomplish several things. It should comfortably accommodate the number of guests, be convenient to get to, allow you to stay within your working budget, and, most important, offer the amenities and assistance you'll need for the event.

What kind of atmosphere, environment, and setting do you visualize? Is it an indoor party or an outdoor celebration? How many guests do you anticipate? Choosing a location that best suits these variables will help you make a final choice. Depending on your individual needs, you can really customize your party to your budget. Sometimes what initially appears to be less expensive, such as hosting a party at home, can end up costing more than a rented space that has been designed to accommodate every detail. When I ask these important questions of my clients, I know there are specific venues that will serve all our needs and allow for an unforgettable and breathtaking affair. I have produced beautiful galas in newly constructed parking garages, and I have made a simple suburban backyard look, smell, and sound like Paris.

Thinking outside the traditional avenues will help in creating a remarkable event, but it can also be more work. If you have the vision, and cost is not a major concern, anything is possible. But style can be grand even on a limited budget, and there is no substitute for simple good taste. As an event producer I assess the client's desired outcome and balance it with the logistics necessary to achieve those results. My experience over the years has taught me the kind of space that will work best for almost every type of party, large and small. To assist you in making the right decision for your event, I have discussed below the most commonly used locations.

HOTELS

A hotel is a great choice for an event because for the most part it's one-stop shopping. It provides most of the necessary elements needed to help make your event a success. There is an enormous amount of anxiety when hosting your own party, and selecting a hotel is one of the best ways to diminish that anxiety. Whether booking a large ballroom, a meeting or conference room, a suite, or some other space, you are provided with all the in-house amenities. When a hotel provides a cost estimate for its catering service, the price usually includes food and liquor as well as china, flatware, crystal, linens, tables, and chairs. If these items are not included in your package, negotiate with the catering manager for

*H*appy guests make a fabulous party. If you are expecting many out-of-town guests for your party, here are some helpful tips to keep them comfortable and happy:

Upon checking in to the hotel, guests should be greeted with a gift package to let them know how thankful you are that they chose to attend. Make sure you design this welcome package with some type of logo that depicts the festive gathering, such as a printed duffel bag recalling the event: "Jamie and David's wedding, May 25, 2001."

It is always wonderful to include an itinerary of the weekend's events so guests know exactly where and when they are expected.

A map of the area that shows how guests are being transported from one event to the next is also a nice touch.

Provide a list of your favorite places to eat in the area as well as a sightseeing guide to local points of interest.

It is also a good idea to provide a list of local hair salons. This will allow guests who wish to have their hair and makeup done for the party easy access to local professionals.

A midnight snack nestled on your guest's pillow is an easy and appreciated touch. You might consider a small box filled with teas, mints, and even some cookies. Attach a welcome note for an extra-personal touch.

Individual canopies over guests' tables create a more intimate setting within an otherwise cavernous hotel ballroom.

a flat fee per person to encompass these items. Nickels and dimes belong in your piggy bank, not in the pocket of the hotel.

Most hotels will allow you to bring in your own decor, including any theme-oriented decorative fixtures, lighting, floral arrangements, entertainment, additional staging if desired, and linens if their selection is not to your liking. There will be additional costs for these that must be factored into your budget.

Hotels sometimes offer in-house help in planning your event as part of their service. Just remember: You get what you pay for. Now don't get me wrong. There are a lot of very talented hotel staff members who know their particular space better than anyone else does. But I have found that they lack the ability to think beyond those four walls. If given the choice, every party these employees plan would look, feel, and taste the same. My job is to assist in taking events into new frontiers, and in the process I motivate the hotel staff to go beyond the limits. Very often I end up hiring the *talented* catering managers to help run events for me when I'm not physically able to be there.

If you book your party in a hotel, make sure all the outside vendors you have hired are known and trusted people and work well with each other. Be very clear about your expectations, without squelching their creativity. Once the planning is done, let the vendors you've hired and trusted run your party.

CAROLE STATLAND
DIRECTOR OF CATERING
PARK HYATT HOTEL, WASHINGTON, DC

The advantage of booking an event in a smaller hotel is that you will immediately feel like you are in a more intimate dining setting.

DEANNA MADDALENA
HOTEL BEL AIR
LOS ANGELES, CA

HOTEL CHECKLIST When reserving a hotel for an event, there are several important questions to ask:

1. Is the hotel space available on the date you've chosen? The more lead time you have to plan your party, the more likely you are to get the date of your choice at a hotel. It's a good idea to have some alternate dates just in case the hotel is already booked on the date you've selected. Flexibility on this key element will be very helpful in getting the space you want.

2. What is the estimated number of guests the room can fit comfortably? The size of the room is crucial. Too much space or too little space can ruin the party. There is nothing worse than a huge, empty-looking space—except, of course, an overcrowded, cramped space.

3. What limitations are there when installing a themed decor, including staging, lighting, and other special elements for your event? Many of my clients choose an elaborate decorating package that requires time in advance of the event for proper installation. For a basic setup in a hotel ballroom, plan to have about three hours of prep time to pull the room together.

4. What restrictions are not mentioned in the contract? For example, catering restrictions may prevent you from bringing in a kosher

TUTERA TIP: Find out who the photographers are that work best at the hotel. Your pictures will turn out better because they know all the little secret areas.

A silver-beaded charger plate adds a contemporary touch to this refined table setting.

caterer; liquor restrictions may not allow you to bring in an upgraded selection of premium liquors and wines.

5. What kind of party is happening in your space just before your event? Many times you can share the same elements, such as lighting packages or specialty rentals with the previous party host and save a lot of money in the process.

6. How many other events will be taking place in the hotel during your event? If there are other parties planned, visit the hotel on an active night to see if there are any sound or privacy issues. You don't want another party drowning out your special night. I suggest finding a space where nothing else can interfere with your plans. There are too many potential problems when a hotel overbooks the party rooms. Trust me: A bride does not want to share her most important day with the local high school prom.

Here are additional points to consider before booking the space:

1. Never sign on the dotted line until you have personally spoken with at least three other people who have hosted parties at the hotel. (This is true for any venue you are thinking about booking.) Ask them about their experiences: Did everything go according to expectations? How smoothly did things run? What about the quality of the food service and decor? Did anything unexpected occur?

2. Make sure you have sampled the food at the hotel before booking the space. In the planning business this is referred to as a "tasting." If a hotel declines to prepare a tasting, book the party elsewhere. The night of your party is the wrong time to discover that the food is not to your liking. This is also an opportunity to experience the service and overall environment. It is extremely important to see how the hotel handles its events, and firsthand experience is the best indicator of how your event will be.

3. Be prepared for additional fees such as overtime, cleanup charges, electrical hookups, and union charges. Most hosts are not made aware of the hotel's union status before getting stuck with unexpected expenses. Ask your catering manager in advance about these additional fees.

4. Coat check fees and parking fees are additional costs. Some hosts choose to pay for them, while others allow their guests to bear the expense. This is important! All tipping, parking, and coat check fees should be paid by the host. It is definitely noticed by guests and always appreciated. As far as I'm concerned, this is not an area to save money.

TENTED PARTIES

A tented party can take place almost anywhere, but not every backyard or outdoor area can handle a tented party. I've tented parking lots, backyards, pools, streets, fields, valleys, and beaches, coast to coast. To me, a tented party offers a blank canvas. If given the choice between a ballroom and a tented space, I'll always go for the tent. The ability to create a more customized look and feel is much greater with a tented space because you start from the ground up—literally.

Remember that hiring tenting professionals will help guarantee a successful fete. But be warned that this can result in the highest level of stress a host can endure. If you know what you're doing, for the most part you can control everything except the weather. We've all heard the nightmare stories of tents that leak, blow away, and even collapse on the crowd. (Note: For fun-filled tent disasters, rent the movies *Betsy's Wedding* and *Father of the Bride*.) Being under a tent that leaks or that is not secure can immediately ruin a party, not to mention your shoes. Oh, and it can also be very dangerous. This is simply not a risk worth taking, so make sure you complete a thorough site inspection before committing to a tented party.

It is extremely important to work with a professional company if you are planning a tented event. Parties have increased in size and complexity; therefore, it's important to coordinate a team that can work together for your greatest success.

TUTERA TIP: When considering a public venue as a possible location, such as a museum or library, remember that in most cases it is used by the public during specific hours. Make sure you check the access and availability for setting up your affair.

*H*aving your party at a large hotel can be convenient, but if it is too large, your guests may become confused about where they belong. Yes, my darlings, it happens. One night two guests from another party strolled into an event of mine and started dancing up a storm. They were a regular Ginger Rogers and Fred Astaire—except that they were at the wrong party. Apparently they had gone to the bathroom to put on their dancing shoes, and when they returned, they made a left when they should have made a right and ended up on my bride and groom's dance floor. The bride approached me and asked if I knew who these two "dancing fools" were. I shook my head in confusion and said, "They're not friends of yours?" Eventually I was left to politely shuffle them off to Buffalo while they never missed a beat.

Go into a tented party with your eyes open. Building a tent is general contracting. It's like building any addition to your home. A professional tent company must be familiar with building codes. The company you choose to work with should provide the tent, the shell to be built upon, special carpets and dance floors, special flooring that is built up to level uneven ground, different elevations if required, electrical services, and heating and air conditioning if needed. The price of a tent and the equipment is pretty much the same whether your budget is large or small. The details and the amount of labor at the site will drive the price up considerably. Budgets are based on time and materials, so it's important to be as straightforward with your tent contractor as possible in the early stage of planning to keep your budget under control. Every major player is a member of a tent association. I always recommend those members because I know they are capable of producing major events in various locations.

Tents can be used with no walls or with retractable flaps allowing for a breeze or protection from rain and dampness as well as privacy. In warmer months, they can become very hot inside without proper ventilation.

There are a lot of criteria we use when judging the appropriate size of a tent for an event. The standard guideline is 15–17 square feet per person. A sit-down meal with no dancing is 10 square feet per person. If a sit-down meal is going to be served and there will be dancing, we use a 15-square-foot-per-person measurement. If it is a stand-up cocktail party with more than one bar and minimal seating, we use what is called a gallery space, approximately 6 square feet per person. Seating for a tented ceremony requires at least 7 square feet per person plus additional space for aisles and altars. Some events, such as a cabaret-style club including a stage area, dancing, and lounge areas, can be 20 square feet per person or more.

CHRIS STARR
STARR TENTS, NEW YORK

I couldn't have said it better myself! The quality of information you give to your contractor will impact the outcome positively or negatively, so it is important to work out the details as far in advance as you can if you are planning a tented affair. Deadlines for parties rarely change, and building a tent doesn't have the same flexibility as other

construction jobs to be complete. I encourage my clients to ask the contracted tent company to provide an on-site foreman during the event in case there are any unexpected glitches. Tented parties are a major production, but if you work with a team of professionals, the benefits offer a relaxed and stress-free experience for you as the host.

TENTED PARTY CHECKLIST Several questions should be asked when making the decision to host a tented party:

1. Is your property capable of having an outdoor party? Have a professional do a complete site inspection of your property. Not all properties can handle a tented event. Many of my clients have had dreams of a backyard wedding, but they live in New York City. I can create that same outdoor feeling by having the wedding at a conservatory or renting a home in the suburbs.

2. Is there ample space for parking guests' cars? Valet service is a must for a formal affair, and I often suggest it for a tented event. Contract with a valet parking service. You are entrusting your guests' cars to strangers; therefore, make sure the valet parking company has proper insurance, and check the recommendations they provide. When using a valet service, it is important to keep traffic flowing quickly and smoothly. I have been a guest at many parties where the valet company has lost keys or reclaim ticket stubs. Waiting a long time for a lost car is not the way you want your guests to remember your party.

3. Is there room for your caterer to prepare and serve the meal? The caterer will need to have either a cook tent attached to the main dining tent or sufficient workspace in a guesthouse, garage, indoor kitchen, or other suitable space.

4. What will be the total cost? Tented parties can tend to cost more than you might think. Since you're creating everything from the ground up, be prepared for many unexpected expenses. Remember, nothing is provided, so you have to bring everything in, including the kitchen sink. You must provide the following elements to host a successful tented affair:

    ▪ Lighting
    ▪ Flooring, carpet, dance floor
    ▪ Rentals (tables, chairs, china, etc.)
    ▪ Staging
    ▪ Air conditioning or heating (sometimes both)

5. How much electrical power is needed? Make sure the proper amount is available. I always insist on having a backup generator

on the site for my clients—or two hundred flashlights;
hey, you never know! This will cover all emergencies
should there be a loss of power. Since power will be dis-
tributed to the caterer, the entertainment, and the lighting vendor, it is crucial to make sure the generator can
accommodate all their needs. Get their requirements in
advance to guarantee proper voltage.

6. Is a permit needed? Most communities require one for
    tenting. The host needs to check with local, city, and/or
    town ordinances. Communities have different require-
    ments, so make sure this is not overlooked.

7. What signage denoting emergency exits is required?
    Find out how many fire extinguishers are needed per
    square foot. Don't be surprised if the local fire marshal makes a
    visit during your event to inspect the property. If the required
    signs are not in place, he will shut the party down immediately.

8. Are there regulations regarding open flames in a tented space?
    Using candles in tents is definitely a gorgeous look, but check to
    see what the community's requirements are before deciding to
    use them for your party. For example, parties I produced in Los
    Angeles and Las Vegas required that all material used be flame-
    proofed in advance.

*Using a tone-on-tone design
in white (white lilies, candles,
tablecloths) created an understated and elegant look within
this billowy white tent.*

PRIVATE HOMES

Your home (or a rented residence) is one of the most intimate settings
to have a party. It is a place where you can invite your friends and
family to be a part of the more private side of you. In the case of a
rented residence, I often suggest that my clients look for a property
that reflects who they are and their ideas of a dream home. Rented
properties are usually grander and more luxurious than our own
homes, so it's an opportunity to be like Cinderella, if only for the night.
Castles, mansions, beachfront homes, villas, country homes, city loft
spaces, yachts—you name it, and it exists for the taking. In New York
City, *Locations* magazine is a great resource to use when searching
for a unique property for your affair. It lists dozens of properties available for rental with a photograph of each location, the amenities
offered, and other pertinent information. It also lists yacht brokers and

25

special event facilities. Similar publications can be found in most metropolitan areas, so check your local newsstand, bookstore, or library.

CHECKLIST FOR RENTING A HOME OR OTHER PROPERTY

1. Make sure the legal capacity is large enough for your party.

2. If you're renting someone's home, make sure all the amenities are included in the price.

3. Find out whether you must use an in-house caterer or can bring in your own team of event professionals.

4. Explore what other events might be happening that same weekend and what kind of restrictions might be placed on your access to the property both before and after your event.

5. See if the china, silverware, linens, and stemware available from the facility are acceptable to you.

6. Make sure the home you are renting carries all necessary liability and personal injury insurance and that you are covered under that policy for the event. All vendors hired to work on the property must also have their own insurance coverage.

CHECKLIST FOR PREPARING THE INTERIOR OF YOUR OWN HOME

1. De-clutter your party space. Remove all unnecessary items from coffee tables, bookshelves, magazine racks, and especially the floor. This removal process helps create an easier and more accessible space for a better flow of traffic throughout the party.

2. Make sure your furniture is in good condition. Tables and chairs that wobble are accidents waiting to happen. This preparation time is a perfect opportunity to attend to those little things that need fixing.

3. Wait until after the party to make *major* improvements to the interior. People usually think it's important to spruce up their home in advance of the party by putting a fresh coat of paint on the walls and cleaning the carpets. I encourage my clients to wait until after

the party to make these improvements. However, freshening up the place by removing scuffs from the walls and spot-cleaning carpeting or rugs can help give the appearance a boost.

4. Don't overlook any room in the house that might be considered off-limits to guests. Someone will always wander into that "private" space, whether you know it or not. The kids need to clean their rooms, and the basement, garage, home office, etc., all need to be tidied as well.

5. Give extra attention to the cleanliness of bathrooms and kitchens. Tubs, toilets, sinks, and floors should be immaculate. The chrome should shine like the top of Mr. Clean's head! Make sure the bathrooms are well stocked with extra hand towels. I prefer to place elegant paper hand towels and liquid soap in every bathroom so each guest has the availability of fresh towels and soap. Light a fragrant candle or place potpourri to disguise any odors. Perfume, lipstick, a hairbrush, and even mouthwash are always nice to have available if they don't clutter the space.

6. The kitchen is ground zero for a party at home. It is the control center from which every detail is overseen and administered. Therefore, it should be well organized and spotless.

7. Once everything has been put in its proper place, a final dusting and vacuuming will help give the entire home a fresh, clean appearance.

8. Make sure you have enough space to hang up your guests' coats. You can rent a coat rack (or buy one) for very little money. Don't forget extra hangers. The old "throw your coat on the bed" trick just isn't cool anymore unless you're in college. As hard is it might be to admit, your frat party days are over!

If you have an open kitchen, you can use the countertop to set up a buffet—but only if no significant food preparation for the event needs to take place in the kitchen.

PREPARING THE EXTERIOR The amount of preparation the outside of your home needs depends on the time of year, the climate in which you live, and the look you are going for. The best advice I can offer is to survey the entire property and decide what needs the most attention. If you notice something wrong, your guests are also sure to notice. Whether you are going for a tidy look or something more lavish, if you use a gardener or lawn service, consult with them about what needs to be done and how far in advance you should plan to make these improvements so that they last until the big day.

CHECKLIST FOR PREPARING
THE EXTERIOR OF YOUR HOME

1. Although it is not necessary, fresh paint always gives a home a clean appearance, but it is not something you have to do unless you were planning to paint anyway.

2. Make sure your address is easy to find. If there is no number on your home, be sure to mark the property with something that identifies it as the right place, especially at night, such as balloons, luminaries, a stork—anything that says, "The party is here!"

3. Updating that beat-up picnic table and those cracked plastic chairs is always a good idea. Conversely, it's never a good idea to let guests leave with a splinter from worn wooden patio furniture.

4. Even though you may be raising the next Michael Jordan, remove the portable basketball net and all other movable children's toys. An exception to this is if you're having young children over for an afternoon get-together. Put the toys in a designated child's play area for their enjoyment, but don't let them detract from the adult festivities.

5. Raking leaves and mowing the lawn are essential, but never cut the lawn the day of the party. Allergies plus fresh clippings can make for a real mess.

6. Burn citronella candles or tiki torches to avoid bugs, especially in the spring and summer months. If you are having a larger party or have very large property, you might want to have the area sprayed a few days ahead of time.

7. Parties that start in the early evening and go into the night should have some sort of outdoor lighting that can be controlled as darkness sets in.

I discourage my clients from making major changes to the environment or decor. It is unnecessary if you know how to utilize the assets already in your home. Formal or informal, your guests should always feel at home in your home. Gone are the days of plastic coverings over the formal furniture— thank goodness! But here to stay is the chic slipcovered look designed to take a beating. Using slipcovers is a good way to freshen up the look of any room in your home and to spruce up even the most weathered and worn furniture. Slipcovers are usually washable and can be used over and over.

8. If you have a pool or hot tub, make sure there is a safety gate, especially if you are expecting young children. The pool and/or hot tub should be serviced the day of the party. If you are planning to use the pool during the party, make sure enough time has passed between the pool maintenance and swimming.

9. Consider your pet's feelings as well as your guests' when deciding whether or not to include your family pet in the fun. Large crowds can overwhelm animals, and they can become irritable and unpredictable. Consider a pet hotel or a neighbor who might not be attending the event to watch your animal for the night. It is truly in everyone's best interest.

PARKING AT A PRIVATE HOME Hire a valet parking service for larger gatherings and make sure you do not allow your guests to tip. Valet parking makes attending a party more convenient for your guests. I highly recommend that you ensure enough room for your guests to park as near to your home as possible. Remove your own vehicles from your driveway by parking them in the garage or down the street. Your guests should never be inconvenienced by a long walk, especially when it is a more formal gathering. John Dent of Advanced Parking Concepts, an expert on the important things you should know when hiring a valet parking company, offered the following helpful advice:

> Hire a company that is experienced in providing special event parking service. A company that provides valet service to restaurants or nightclubs is not necessarily prepared for handling a residential special event. Make sure the company inspects the site before the party to work out the logistics in advance. Each situation is different. An experienced company will provide the host (or event coordinator) with a plan of operation that includes where the guests will be greeted, where the cars are going to be parked, time of valet arrival and departure, the number of staff (a minimum of one valet for every ten to fifteen cars), how the staff will be attired, and insurance requirements. As a host you should request a certificate of insurance naming you (and your spouse) as additional insured on that policy for the date of your event.
>
> JOHN DENT
> ADVANCED PARKING CONCEPTS
> VERONA, NJ

TUTERA TIP: The best parties should arouse every sense. Aromas, such as scented candles, potpourri, and the smell of food cooking help create an ambience that entices guests. Here's a recipe for citrus potpourri: Slice fresh lemons, oranges, limes, cloves, and cinnamon sticks, place in a pot, and simmer over low heat. Let the aroma permeate the whole house.

OVERLEAF *A casual outdoor lunch is set beneath the shade of an arbor for the guests' comfort.*

Be considerate of neighbors if you know you will have an abundance of vehicles on the streets surrounding your home. If anyone asks you not to park in front of his or her home, be respectful. In most cases I encourage my clients to drop a note and sometimes a small gift such as a fruit basket at a neighbor's home with the explanation that there is a party planned, giving the date and expected duration.

RESTAURANTS AND PRIVATE CLUBS

Restaurants are an easy alternative to entertaining at home and can be more intimate than a hotel. Many restaurants have private rooms available for rent, and some will even allow you to take over the entire place for the night. But do your research. Restaurants that are not accustomed to having parties are a risky choice for a special event. Serving individual tables is sometimes a smoother process than serving one large group, so make sure the staff and kitchen are equipped to handle your guests. Events that work well in a restaurant setting tend to be smaller, such as bridal showers, company dinners, intimate holiday gatherings, bachelor/bachelorette parties, birthday and anniversary dinners, and retirement parties.

If you are planning a party at a private club such as a country club or social club, you should follow the advice offered previously concerning a party at a hotel. Generally, the management at a club is used to private events, so a party at such a facility should be a smooth experience. Private clubs also allow you to work with an outside planner, but their guidelines may be stricter than that of hotels or other venues. Make sure that you stay within the bylaws of the club so that you remain in good standing if you are a member. If you are not a member of the club but someone has sponsored you for the event, it is even more important to follow all rules and remain gracious when hosting in that facility.

CHECKLIST FOR RENTING A RESTAURANT OR PRIVATE CLUB

1. Find out the history of parties hosted at the restaurant you're considering well in advance. Get references and check them out.

2. Unlike hotels, restaurants often limit the menu selection to a few main dishes that are easy to serve en masse. You'll want to sit

with the manager and plan a menu, do a tasting, and be certain that you like the presentation.

3. Timing and service are the two biggest complaints from clients who have experienced a gathering at a restaurant. These two pitfalls can be avoided if you create a well-thought-out plan far enough in advance. It is sometimes a good idea to write a service schedule that gives the exact time each course should be served. It helps keep the staff on track, and things run more smoothly.

4. You can suggest that the staff wear particular clothes so they are easily identified as staff by the guests; the clothes can be tuxedos, black pants and white shirts, or long white chef's aprons.

5. Find out about any time restrictions for accessing the restaurant and other limitations. Some small towns require that alcohol consumption be limited and discontinued at a specific time.

6. Most restaurants will not allow you to bring in your own liquor, though some allow you to bring upgraded wine or champagne. Check on the liquor restrictions beforehand.

7. Make parking arrangements in advance. If the restaurant uses a valet service, I suggest using their service. If they don't, check on the accessibility of parking in the immediate area. Make it as easy and convenient for your guests as possible.

8. As I've commented previously, your guests should never have to reach into their own pockets at any point in the party. This means no cash bars, no tipping, no coat check fee, and no splitting the bill!

When selecting a venue, it is important that the space reflect the style and personality of both the event and the honoree.

DAVID STARLING
CIPRIANI'S 42ND STREET
NEW YORK, NY

HOW TO PICK A PARTY PLANNER

A party planner wears many hats when it comes to helping a client arrange for an event—part planner, part psychiatrist, part referee, and your new best friend. Let me fill you in on a little secret: It's our job to help you feel comfortable. I'll go to dress fittings, hair and makeup consultations, food tastings, nightclubs to listen to bands (which I

33
—

eventually may talk you out of), and whatever else it takes to pull off the event of your dreams. I've even taken a nervous groom out for cocktails just to be certain he will walk down that plank—oops, I mean aisle. The most important advice I can give you about hiring a party and event planner is to follow your instincts. Do you feel comfortable with the person? Can you communicate your desires in an open and friendly dialogue? Does the planner's style mesh with the look you're aiming for in planning your event? You'll know immediately after your first meeting. Trust your instincts. This relationship is an important one, and if you're having any doubts about the person, move on. You won't regret it.

Once you've made the decision to work with a planner, ask your friends and family for recommendations. Always check the references of the person you are considering. He or she will be spending your hard-earned dollars, and it's very important to feel you have made the best choice for your needs. When interviewing a planner, assess how organized he or she is. Does the planner present ideas in a well-thought-out manner? If they seem scattered to you, they probably are, and you should ask yourself if that style of working makes you comfortable.

There are four types of party planners you never want to work with or experience firsthand. The first is "no clue Sue." This person has no clue about planning an event, large or small. The second type of planner is "lame lady Lucy." She might be able to pull off a nice party, but do you really want to trust your event to this fashion maven? The third is "last-minute Charlie," who loves to leave all the important details to chance. Finally, there is "fabulous frantic Frank," who is too cool for your event. Here is a simple rule to guide your decision: When it comes to choosing a party planner, you can judge a book by its cover. Ask to see photos of the planner's previous work and, as always, check numerous references.

BUDGET

While everyone throwing a party has a different budget to work with, the goal is to create a wonderful celebration for family, friends, and one's self. There is no set formula to divvying up the budget, but I can advise you about the best ways to do so for your party.

The first rule is to set a working budget. Knowing that you have a certain amount of money set aside to make this dream a reality will help you achieve that goal. Whether you've planned for $5,000 or $50,000, the money must be spread out to cover all your needs. Establishing that dollar amount in advance is the biggest hurdle. The husband of a client recently called me after I had submitted my proposal for their daughter's wedding. He said, "I'm not adding an addition to my house, I'm giving a wedding!" Needless to say, he considered the numbers frightening and intimidating. He had a number clearly in mind that he wanted to spend but didn't realize what the actual costs would be. I explained to him that we could readdress their desires and work within the limits he was comfortable with and still be able to plan a beautiful affair for his "little girl." We went through the budget, decided on three main areas of importance, and focused the finances on achieving success in those areas.

When planning any event, the host needs to decide what areas are the most important. For example, if entertainment is important to you, allocate a little more money for it and less on lighting. Being realistic is definitely helpful when melding your fantasy and reality. If your budget doesn't allow for a formal sit-down dinner, you might want to consider a cocktail party instead. A fabulous cocktail party can be as much if not more fun and fabulous than a formal dinner. Do not allow your creativity to be controlled by the dollar. Sometimes the client who comes to me with a lower budget gets the more creative party. Anyone can spend a lot of money on a party, if they have it to spend.

A party is memorable for many reasons. The occasion, the guests, and the hosts are just a few reasons that someone might remember a party—and they have absolutely nothing to do with money. My intention when it came to writing this book was to help you select the best of my trade secrets to help you make your event—grand or intimate, and no matter what size—work for you on any budget.

Food and location are the two budget hogs; they usually take the biggest bite out of the planned estimate. Depending on your preferences, the third item is the great unknown and will be determined by your needs. Certain fees are set regardless of the number of guests. A band is one price whether twenty people or two hundred people are in attendance. However, the number of people you host

Doubling up certain elements of your décor can add up to significant savings in your budget. This beautiful large floral arrangement was initially used as ceremony décor and then moved to embellish the place-card table.

tremendously affects the money allocated for food and liquor. Knowing your head count in advance will help reduce unexpected last-minute increases in the budget, and there are always last-minute surprises that affect the budget!

If you are working with an event planner, chances are that person will handle all the business aspects associated with every contracted vendor. If you are not working with a planner, you will be the one entering into each agreement. There are some basic guidelines to follow when negotiating and signing these contracts. By following them, you will save time and money, and avoid any surprises down the road.

- Be honest about your expectations and limitations. Let each vendor know up front what your working budget is. This direct and honest approach will save everyone a lot of time and hassle.

- Educate yourself by obtaining several price quotes from various vendors, but never submit one vendor's proposal to another.

- Make sure you have a sense of comfort with the vendor you choose to work with even if his or her fees are slightly higher. That peace of mind is worth a few extra dollars.

- Get your agreement with every vendor in writing. This is the best way to guarantee that you will have everything you expect on the day of your party.

- Each contract should include a list of the services being provided, the costs, the date of the event, the starting time, the duration of the party, and the cancellation policies.

- Contracts should always include a schedule for payment. Every vendor has individual requirements. The schedule will clearly state the date and amount due.

- Most vendors ask for a deposit, and there is usually a strict cancellation policy that requires a full or partial forfeiture of the money on deposit.

- Contracts should state any time restrictions that might limit access for that vendor.

- Overtime is the most frequently questioned addition to a bill. A party that runs long or requires additional time to tear down can add significantly to the final bills. Be very clear about what these rates are in advance so there are no surprises at the end of a wonderful event.

- Be sure both parties sign every contract. An unexecuted agreement is not valid. Put a copy in your files.

- Beware of costs defined in contracts as "miscellaneous expenses." Ask the vendor to define the items that usually fall into this category and be certain that they are acceptable to you.

- Never assume anything when it comes to contracts. Be sure all your concerns have been addressed and are clearly stated in writing.

- Remember that you are planning a fun event, but you are still doing business with everyone you hire. Treat each transaction as such. Be polite with your vendors. You will always get more flies with honey than with vinegar.

I always tell my clients that it's very easy to get swept up by the excitement of the planning process and overlook some of the less enjoyable aspects, such as contracts. But the business side of the process must be dealt with and, if handled properly, will save much angst.

Everything discussed in this chapter is intended to help you get started on your party plans. No matter what kind of party it is, selecting the date, choosing a location, and securing it are the essential first steps in making the event become a reality. Nothing else can be arranged or confirmed until these are taken care of. Once the date and location are determined, the rest of your plans should come together relatively easily. The next step is to let people know you're planning a party!

Laura Leigh

and

Paul Blair Brown

request the pleasure of your company
at the celebration of their marriage

Sunday, the eleventh of February
Two thousand and one
at six o'clock in the evening

Amelia Island Resort
Amelia Island, Florida

2 | Invitations

The proper selection of guests is the first essential
in all entertaining. Taste in home furnishings or in clothes
or in selecting a cook is nothing compared to taste in people!

—EMILY POST

When your guests receive the invitation to your party, it should set the tone for the entire affair. The more formal the invitation, the more formal the event. I've had a lot of fun with clients who were willing to get creative and send out an invitation that stretched our imaginations. When guests receive an invitation, they formulate an opinion about the type of party they're being invited to. The outside of the envelope, the stamps used, the layout of the invitation, and the type used—all the details count. A great invitation creates curiosity and intrigue. If you want to really grab the attention of your guests, create an invitation that guarantees the impression that this is a party *not* to be missed.

The elaborate invitation to this garden-themed wedding was centered on a lattice frame and finished with a pretty ribbon.

THE GUEST LIST

It's a good idea to create a guest list in advance. A party is about being with people you like to be around, and inviting guests out of guilt simply takes the fun out of it. There are circumstances that require an

39

obligatory invitation here and there, such as a business function or party in honor of someone else. But when hosting your own party, the idea is to surround yourself with the people who mean the most to you and with whom you want to share this special time.

Compiling a guest list serves several purposes. It allows you to get an idea of the number of people who might attend and how many invitations you'll need. When making a guest list, remember that Mr. and Mrs. Smith may count as two people, but only one invitation is needed. Many of my clients have forgotten this mathematical equation when giving me their final count and then couldn't figure out why they had one hundred extra invitations.

Make sure you have complete and current address information and the correct titles and spellings of your guests' names, such as Dr. and Mrs. Freud or Mr. Brad Pitt and Ms. Jennifer Aniston. Be sure to address the invitations properly.

When making your guest list, you must decide whether your single friends and family members will be invited with a guest. I am often asked what is correct regarding this issue. I generally encourage my clients to invite singles to bring guests unless it becomes a budgetary issue or physical space is extremely limited for the event. Whatever you decide, make sure the envelope of the invitation clearly expresses what you want.

Create a master invitation guest list organizer. This will help you keep track of your RSVPs, and you can use it to record any gifts you receive. It will also be helpful when it comes to writing thank-you notes. Simply indicate by using a check mark for each category.

Name(s) _____

_____

Invitation sent _____ RSVP received _____ Number in party _____

Address _____

_____

Gift _____

Telephone number _____ Email _____

Thank-you written _____ Thank-you sent _____

If you are planning a wedding, remember that there are two sets of parents and that two guest lists must be merged together into one. The bride and groom must openly discuss this issue early to avoid any unnecessary and unwanted conflict. Filing for divorce *before* the wedding is never a good idea.

INVITATION ESSENTIALS

Regardless of how creative you get with your invitations, they must contain the following essential information: the date, time, location, occasion, and host's name. It is also nice to include a suggested style of dress and other information such as directions, how to RSVP, whether the event is a surprise for the honored guest, names and numbers of nearby hotels, and parking advice. A properly written invitation will help eliminate a flurry of phone calls from guests seeking more details. Guests will still call, of course, but they'll probably be complimenting you on how fabulous the invitation looks instead of being confused!

The invitation for this birthday celebration was sent to each guest as a wrapped gift box filled with confetti.

INVITATION CHECKLIST

1. **Date.** Make sure you've established the date and location before getting the invitations printed.

2. **Location.** Give the location directions to your guests by inserting them in the invitation. If you have more than one location—such as a wedding ceremony at a church and the reception immediately following at another location—be sure the details are conveyed in the invitation. If you are providing transportation to and from any locations, that should be included as well.

3. **Time.** The proper time for your party will vary depending on the occasion. More formal events tend to be evening affairs, while less formal parties can be scheduled for early or late afternoon.

4. Wedding invitations usually ask guests to arrive thirty minutes prior to the actual ceremony.

5. Certain religions have time restrictions for ceremonies, so check with your clergy about what is appropriate.

6. For casual events such as barbecues, beach parties, clambakes, and Super Bowl parties, there is no formality about the time. I call these types of parties "fly-bys" because many people attend more than one.

7. If it is important for your guests to arrive promptly at a particular time, make that very clear in the invitation. I plan a lot of events on yachts, and once the ship sails, it's too late!

8. **Occasion.** Let your guests know what the occasion is. This may appear simple, but you'd be surprised at how easy it is to overlook, especially when you are trying to be creative. A friend of mine was having a birthday party, and in writing a poem for the text of the invitation, she inadvertently left out what the occasion was. Upon receiving this cute and clever invitation, I phoned to ask her what we were celebrating. She was horrified because nowhere on the invitation did it say it was her birthday—but it did say to bring presents!

For a sweet sixteen party, a sixties theme ran throughout the invitation, the RSVP card, and the place cards, which were designed as VIP passes.

The invitation photograph includes the following calligraphy text:

Please share in our happiness when, in the tradition of his ancestors, our son **Brandon** is called to the Torah as a Bar Mitzvah Saturday, the seventeenth of April Nineteen hundred and ninety-nine five-thirty in the evening Washington Hebrew Congregation Washington, District of Columbia

Lyn and Barry Chasen

Transportation will be provided from Washington Hebrew Congregation to The Park Hyatt Please plan to pick your child up at 12:00 a.m.

Brandon's Celebration Continues... With Dinner & Dancing The Park Hyatt Washington, District of Columbia Black Tie

We look forward to having you Please respond by the twenti...

9. If you are throwing a surprise party, make sure it is very clear on the invitation that it is a SURPRISE party!

10. **Hosts.** How to word who is hosting the party is very tricky and should be carefully considered, especially when dealing with divorced parents who are jointly hosting a party. This issue is raised most frequently when planning weddings, sweet sixteen birthday parties, and bar/bat mitzvahs. I always advise my clients to choose the wording that will make their child and guests feel the most comfortable. Sometimes this works, but other times . . . Have I ever told you about the War of the Roses? I've sat through many brutal arguments, and the truth is, no one wins. It's a party—it's supposed to be fun.

11. For more formal events, protocol suggests that whoever is paying for the party should be listed as the host. If divorced parents are paying equally, the woman is always listed first, and the rat bastard—uh, I mean, the ex-husband—is listed second.

12. **RSVP.** For the record, RSVP is French for répondez s'il vous plaît, or please respond. It is intended to allow you to keep a record of

For slightly less formal events, a rich texture can be added to the invitations if you use imported papers.

43
—
Invitations

who is attending. This is especially useful for the final head count that you must give many of the vendors you're working with prior to the big event.

13. There are several response methods that can be used when sending an invitation. An RSVP requests that your guests reply whether or not they will attend. Enclosing a *response card* asks guests to reply by mail. Response cards should always come with a self-addressed, stamped envelope for the guests' convenience. *Regrets only* on an invitation requires your guests to respond only if they are unable to attend.

14. On every RSVP method, you should include a date by which your guests must reply. This makes planning easier for you.

15. Be prepared for guests who do not respond at all. If you have not received a response from an invited guest by the response date, it is perfectly acceptable to phone the person to get an answer.

16. **Suggested attire.** I prefer to let guests know in advance what the proper attire is for any party, posh or intimate. "White tie" is the most formal evening wear. It generally consists of black tailcoat, wing collar, and white bow tie. It is rarely suggested these days but can be a very elegant look for a formal wedding or dinner party. "Black tie" is standard tuxedo wear. This means evening wear for both men and women. "Festive or creative" attire means—well, who knows what it means? My suggestion is not to use these terms. It's confusing and can be very embarrassing for you and your guests. "Coat and tie," "Jacket required," and "Business attire" all mean pretty much the same thing. Men are in jackets and ties, and women are in comfortable but not formal evening wear. Slacks, skirts, cocktail dresses, and suits are all acceptable. "Casual" attire means nice informal clothes for men and women. Use your judgment based on the party you're attending, the location, and the host's usual style.

17. Despite the popularity of email and other electronic devices, I still firmly believe that an invitation to a party should be sent in an envelope delivered via the U.S. Postal Service. A very informal invitation, such as a "must-see TV" get-together on Thursday night, is the only exception to this rule.

18. It is always nice to coordinate your postage stamps with the occasion. Holiday party invitations should use a holiday stamp. Weddings can use stamps with doves or that read "Love." There are many options available, so visit your post office either in person or on the Internet to check out all the choices.

If you follow these steps, invitation disasters will be averted. If you find that you have inadvertently left someone off your list, simply explain that it was an oversight and make room for the person to attend even if it is last minute. I always find this tactful method smooths even the most ruffled feathers.

SELECTING THE INVITATION

FORMAL

A formal party calls for a formal invitation that is printed, plain, and elegant. I suggest using a heavy stock paper in cream or white with a simple script font, in black ink. There are many possible variations on this basic invitation, such as embossed, engraved, or raised lettering. Decorations might also be added, such as ribbons, bows, or borders. If you are planning a formal affair, let an invitation specialist guide you in your final decisions. There

TUTERA TIP: There are two types of calligraphy to choose from when addressing envelopes for a formal invitation. The first type is pen-and-ink calligraphy, which is printed by hand. The second type is done by computers and replicates the look of handwritten calligraphy. This method is not necessarily less expensive and can sometimes look as if it were done mechanically, thus losing the effect of hand-printed calligraphy. Always ask to see samples of the calligrapher's work.

For formal invitations, it is important to design all elements in a similar style. The invitation to this wedding is at right; at left (from top to bottom) are the program for the ceremony (cover and interior), the table number card and envelope, and the menu card.

is usually no additional charge for this service because you'll be placing the print order anyway.

Allow three to six weeks to receive the invitations from the printer. This means you need to order them six weeks prior to the date you plan to send them out to your guests. Before the delivery of your invitations you will be given a proof from the printer to make any final corrections. Check to make sure every detail is correct.

THEMED

Themed invitations are my personal favorite because they allow the host to be less formal and more creative with the party from the earliest stage. If you are having a themed event, the invitation will mesh with the design and set the mood from the instant the invitation is opened. I've sent invitations in the form of a concert poster in a large round mailing tube, invitations on videotape and compact disc, and invitations with props such as stuffed animals, cigar cases, and baseball hats that coordinated with the theme. Some of my clients have taken the theme to extremes. I planned an over-the-top party for a client who wanted to re-create the red light district in Amsterdam—in his backyard in a suburb of New York City. His invitation asked guests to RSVP to a number where a message, recorded in a heavy Dutch accent, provided the party details. From the moment they received the invitation, the guests knew this was no ordinary backyard garden party. The more elaborate the invitation, the more time you should allow for receiving and reviewing proofs from the printer. Remember

The invitations and place cards for this party reveal the circumstances behind the event—my client was starting a major construction project at his new home and he wanted to celebrate.

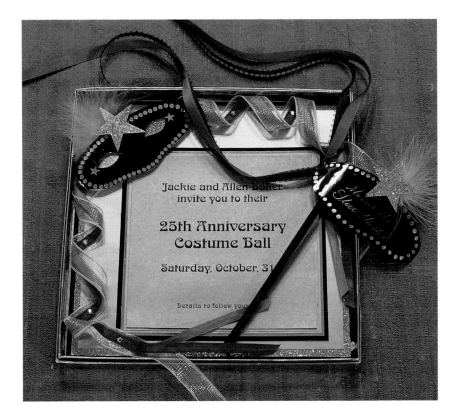

Jackie and Allen Bonet
invite you to their

**25th Anniversary
Costume Ball**

Saturday, October, 31

Details to follow your

*To get guests excited about an
upcoming masquerade party,
one host incorporated a mask
into the invitation.*

that extraordinary invitations will be more expensive in every way,
from design to construction and postage. Those costs must be factored into your budget.

INFORMAL

There are numerous options for creating an informal invitation, many of
which are inexpensive alternatives that still look beautiful. Stationery
stores carry a wide selection of stationery and preprinted invitations.
Blank stationery allows you to print the invitations on your home com-
puter or use a professional printing service. Either way, you'll need to
think about how you want the invitation to read and be certain of your
choice before you go to print. Preprinted invitations with fill-in-the-blank
information lines are easily filled in by hand, using a calligraphy pen that
won't smear; they may also be printed if properly typeset.

> **Invitations must reflect the personal spirit and style of the
> individual hosting the party. It is important to create an invita-
> tion that reflects the formality or casualness of the affair.**
>
> LAURA LEIGH
> ALPINE CREATIVE GROUP
> NEW YORK, NY

PROPER WORDING
FOR EVERY OCCASION

The wording of invitations is a little more complicated these days. With the increasing divorce rate, the nuclear family is now less common. My clients always ask me for help when it comes to proper phrasing, so I have compiled some examples that are comfortable and appropriate for almost every circumstance and occasion.

FORMAL WEDDING INVITATIONS

Mr. and Mrs. George Smith
request the honor of your presence
at the marriage of their daughter
Lisa Marie
to
Mr. Bradley Bierman
on Saturday, the ninth of March
Two Thousand Two
at six o'clock in the evening
The Plaza Hotel
Fifth Avenue
New York, New York
Reception immediately following

This is the most traditional format possible for a wedding invitation. It's perfect if the bride's mother and father are hosting the wedding as a couple.

Mrs. Katherine Renold
Mr. Ralph Renold
request the honor of your presence
at the marriage of their daughter
Emily
to
Mr. Joseph Piplo
on Saturday, the eighth of June
Two Thousand Two
at six o'clock in the evening
The Metropolitan Club
New York, New York

Divorced parents may prefer to have their names on different lines and not linked with the word "and." This is a common way to denote that the parents are divorced.

A Passion for Parties

Mr. and Mrs. Joe Wagner
request the pleasure of your company
for dinner
in honor of
Mr. Tony Griffin
on Friday, the twenty-second of June
Two Thousand One
at eight o'clock in the evening
124 Duck Walk Lane
Southampton, New York
R S V P

212-555-5555
Formal attire

For an informal invitation you may use figures, such as 8:00 and June 21, as opposed to spelling out the numbers. Also, you will want to change the dress code to casual.

Once your invitations are in the mail, the real fun of planning the party can begin. Just remember that when you send out your invitations with enough advance warning, you give everyone enough time to make the proper arrangements to attend your special occasion.

3 | Design Concepts

Creating an atmosphere for your event is easier than you might think. Whether you spend a small fortune or virtually no money at all, you have the same opportunity to create a pleasant, comfortable environment for your guests. If you can visualize the event—the who, what, where, when, and why—you can turn your dream into a reality. The first place any celebration takes on life is in your mind. Like a jigsaw puzzle, it can all come together if you have all the pieces and can see the big picture. They have to fit together to create the final image.

The concepts in this chapter make up most of the visual aspects associated with planning a party. The atmosphere is a culmination of the following elements: theme, lighting, table design, and flowers. Each of these elements is part of the overall picture, regardless of how large or small or how fancy or informal your affair becomes. Romantic dinners for two at home and a large wedding party are equally affected by these four visual elements.

This award-winning table design featured an elaborate napkin treatment with ribbons and flowers that enhanced the elegant place setting.

THEME

Theme parties are fun to plan because you are striving for a particular look and atmosphere. Not every party has to have a theme, but generally there is a purpose for the celebration, such as a birthday or

This table uses simple elements to create a dinner party suffused with Asian influences. Wheat grass, slate, bamboo stalks, and orchid heads create a stunning centerpiece and, combined with elegant lacquered dinnerware, make a perfect setting for. . .take-out Chinese.

anniversary. Even if you're not throwing a "Night in Morocco" party, you still want a special look and feel to create a symmetrical sensation. Striking a balance among the details is always important to creating an overall theme, and it is important to develop the concept through a carefully planned and detailed process. Take a specific motif and build on it.

A good example is a party I planned for the Irvington Institute, a philanthropic organization benefiting the study of immunological research. This client requested a Broadway theme. Everything from rafters to rim followed in the Broadway spirit. The design of each table was based on a different Broadway show. I featured *Mame, La Cage aux Folles, The Man of La Mancha,* and *Showboat,* just to name a few. The party took place in The Four Seasons restaurant in New York City. There were twenty-five tables of ten, which meant that twenty-five different Broadway shows were featured. The restaurant has a small pool in the center of the dining room, and I even built a replica of the *Titanic* and sank it in the pool. I used every opportunity to incorporate the Broadway theme into the design elements. I approached the twenty-five tables individually, making it easier to give each one a very particular look. In the overall scheme the twenty-five tables made a terrific combination and gave the entire room a balanced look and theme.

Your invitations should complement the theme. You can decide to send invitations that reflect the theme exactly or simply hint at it to spark the interest and wonderment of your guests.

When your guests enter the party, they should immediately recognize what the theme of the party is. Being creative is important, but confusing the partygoers detracts from the fun. Allow the design to flow and be clean in appearance. You can still create an elaborate decor, but make each detail crisp, clear, and concise.

There are many ways other than decorating a room to incorporate the theme in your party. Remember that successful themes work only if you think outside the proverbial party box and visualize things as larger than life. The following tips will help you incorporate the theme in your next event.

Each table at a Broadway-themed luncheon was decorated with a centerpiece based on a great musical.

1. Have your caterer create a themed food presentation for the first course of your meal. A coconut that has been cracked open and used to hold an exotic first course certainly looks wonderful for a Caribbean party. A single purple orchid can add color and detail. A carved-out miniature pumpkin used to serve a first-course soup is perfect for a harvest- or holiday-influenced theme. Be creative and daring. Incorporating edible flowers into the first course can add color to a springtime event. Beautiful yellow and white edible pansies bring a sweet and fresh look to a wedding table setting These small details are wonderful and usually inexpensive.

2. If you cannot provide specialty place settings such as glassware, flatware, and crystal, you can use a *charger plate* with plain china to add to the style of the theme. An aged copper charger plate or a hammered pewter charger plate is wonderful for a medieval theme party.

3. Flowers, lighting, and overall decoration within the space must reflect the theme. Simply changing the shade or tone of the lighting will alter the entire look. A soft pink light, for example, brings

TUTERA TIP: When planning a theme party, ask children what they think. A child's imagination is always larger than life and can provide inspiration, especially to us bigger kids.

a romantic glow to any setting (and flatters just about everyone). Try a variety of options before making your final decision. Test what looks best in the party space and find a look you like.

SOME FAVORITE THEMES

I always tell people that at an event they should feel as if they're at the theater. Something should be happening all the time, something new to see, hear, taste, and smell. If a show doesn't entertain you, you get bored. The same is true of a party. A party must grab and entertain the guests the entire time of the event. I have planned and produced many unique and original themed parties for clients over the years; these are some of my favorites!

JUNGLE ADVENTURE

I created a jungle environment where guests were transported out of their ordinary everyday world into the depths of the Amazon. I don't mean dot-com. We're talking jungle here, baby. Loin cloths and monkeys. Darkly dyed natural leather shammies were sewn together with leather roping and used as tabletop linen. The centerpieces were a combination of unusual and exotic florals and moss found in tropical regions. Pampas grass, orchids, African protea, and wild grasses decorated tables set for four. Mosquito netting and smilax created a wispy canopy over individual tables, giving an intimate feel to a large party. Large jungle leaves were sewn onto the tablecloths to create a wonderful texture. Natural wood ballroom chairs as well as African masks and artifacts added to the authenticity of the jungle theme and assured that guests would find something new and exciting to look at each moment of the evening.

The jungle theme can be extended to the invitations, place cards, and favors.

A 1930s SUPPER CLUB

Guests entered an all-white tent whose interior was completely transformed into a 1930s supper club. I used a basic black-and-white theme for this party, and created and installed lighting in lavenders, cobalt blues, chocolate brown, amber, and pinks to give a special sparkle. A funky feel was created by mixing four different linen patterns with four different styles of stemware, different base plates, and centerpieces of various heights to add movement and an eclectic feel to the room. Different-styled crystal and antique silver containers held floral arrangements of calla lilies, Casablanca lilies, and gardenias, which were most appropriate for the 1930s supper club theme. The base of the centerpieces had lanterns with black-fringed lampshades and three smaller containers filled with flowers. Fabrics used included charcoal taffeta, silver panne velvet, black panne velvet, organza, and beautiful satins. Drama was created around the perimeter of the tent with 10-by-4-foot panels of the art deco elements taken from the beautiful invitations. Black, gray, and white panels surrounded the tent, along with ten vases 6 feet high filled with huge explosions of Casablanca lilies.

A NIGHT IN AMSTERDAM

I have an incredibly adventurous client who entertains his friends and family once a year with a full-scale bash. One year he outdid himself when he decided to transform his colonial family home into the red-light district of Amsterdam for an extravagant surprise party.

Guests approached a house bathed in vibrant red floodlights and were ushered to the tented backyard by scantily clad men and women. Since the red-light district in Amsterdam is renowned for its legal sex business, we provided props such as whips, handcuffs, and studded collars and placed provocative dancers on stages around the party. The dancers also mingled with the crowd and made sure no one was without a dance partner, while Wycleff Jean performed on a stage constructed on the slate patio terrace. When guests chose to relax, they could do so on black leather and vinyl furniture in intimate lounge areas. Cocktail tables covered in vinyl with chrome studs also lined the dance floor.

My client chose Indonesian food for the evening in keeping with the theme of Amsterdam, which is famous for its Indonesian food. The staff served the classic *rijsttafel* (rice table) with beef, chicken, and shrimp, along with such dishes as steamed vegetables with spicy peanut sauce and curried chicken. A full-service bar was set up at one end of the stage, and the staff passed trays of drinks.

TUTERA TIP: If you are planning a specific themed event, go all the way for complete success. Half a theme is *not* better than no theme at all. It's an all-or-nothing proposition.

55
___
Design Concepts

Bejeweled elegance was added to this menu card by gluing short strands of beads at the top of each card.

ARABIAN NIGHTS

The Arabian night experience began the moment guests entered the room; they were washed in bold colored lighting that I had specially designed. Snake charmers and Arabian belly dancers entertained arriving guests and set the mood for the evening's escape to a foreign land. I transformed an ordinary space into a faraway place using jewel tones, velvet, gold, palms, gold chairs, and walls covered with canvas backdrops of Arabian scenes. Tables were covered with velvet tablecloths. The ceiling was draped in matching colored satin and chiffon. Lavish centerpieces were constructed with bursts of 4-foot-tall palm leaves interspersed with brass, fresh fruits and vegetables, breads, jewels, and colorful candles.

HI-TECH TV TWISTED

Silver tubing spiraled through the ceiling and down to the contemporary structures that were centerpieces on the tables. The centerpieces of glass blocks and aluminum appeared to be floating when viewed against the backdrop of the room that was draped from floor to ceiling in black fabric, creating an illusion of a black hole. Spandex chair covers and tablecloths, bold lighting, and large metal lighting trusses completed the look. The dance floor had a prismatic finish, and when not dancing, guests could view TV monitors displayed in cages around the perimeter of the room.

TUTERA TIP: Use different sizes and shapes of tables to create a unique and eclectic look.

The following are suggestions for other themes:

Tropical Nights	Country Hoedown	Moroccan
Art Deco	Hooray for Hollywood	Carnival
Masquerade	Circus	Broadway
Arabian Nights	Fairy Tale	Sports
Salsa/Latin	Murder Mystery	Fifties Party
Retro	Nautical	Southwestern
New Orleans	Gothic	New York, New York
Renaissance	Roaring Twenties	Greek
Monet's Garden	Asian/Feng Shui	Tuscan
Hawaiian Luau	Midsummer Night's Dream	Caribbean
Disco		

A themed party does not necessarily have to have a specific theme but can simply take on a fresh and unique look. I am often compared to an interior designer. If given the chance, I love to create an entire "look" as a theme. An all-white design is an ethereal, sleek, and peaceful look. It can also be a contemporary or New Age theme. This approach is sometimes more elegant and tasteful than a themed event.

THE TABLE SETTING

How many ways are there to set a table? As many as your mind can create! And like everything that goes into the planning process, a perfect table setting can easily become the focal point for an event. Planning ahead and having an idea of the look you want to create will make the process as seamless as your tablecloths! If I'm planning a party for a client at home, I always start by taking an inventory of what the client already has in stock. I look at the tablecloths, napkins, place mats, runners, platters, service ware, china, stemware, and utensils. I assess what will work and what is needed for the style of party and the number of guests. The goal is to coordinate the color scheme, not to achieve perfectly matched place settings. Color unifies everything, so don't be afraid to mix and match patterns, solids, and items that are not from the same set.

The tablecloth determines the overall look and style of the finished table. It is the blank canvas on which you can create your setting masterpiece. The cloth should hang evenly over every edge of the table. If necessary, use two cloths. You may choose to lay one over the other to create a multilayered look and give added dimension to the table design. I prefer to use simple solid-colored tablecloths or patterned tablecloths of cotton or fine linen, particularly for more formal gatherings. I often use a metallic sheer overlay on top of fine fabrics to add festive glitz and color to a less formal table setting. Store your linens flat, not hanging over a hanger.

When setting a festive table, don't be afraid to play with colors and patterns. You might be surprised at how a bright bold print can change the entire look and feel of your dining room, picnic table, or card table. Sometimes less is more, and sometimes more is more.

Three distinct place settings show how to create dramatically different looks—elegant modern, country chic, or jewel-toned luxury.

*M*aking a tablecloth and matching linens is simple to do and affordable. Go to your local fabric store and choose a fabric whose pattern or design, color, and texture appeals to you. Most fabric stores also sell patterns to help you fit the raw cloth to the size and shape of the table you are using. Make sure you have the proper table dimensions when ordering the fabric so that you purchase enough to make the tablecloth and as many napkins as needed.

———

*T*o remove a stain from a linen or fabric tablecloth, hand wash in warm water using a neutral detergent. Do not use chlorine bleach.

There are no rules. What works is whatever feels right to you and is aesthetically pleasing. It's a party, and having fun is what it's all about. If you are really feeling crafty, you can buy fabric to make matching napkins, draperies, and coverings for your sofas, chairs, lounges, coffee tables, kitchen tables, and even the toilet lids! Creating a look, theme, or design stems from setting a beautiful table.

When setting a less formal table, place mats and runners are often used in place of a linen tablecloth, but only if the table itself is beautiful. Place mats come in many different shapes, sizes, colors, and materials; the possibilities are endless. Mats are generally used for less formal meals and are ideal for protecting expensive tabletops and linens from spills and stains. Again, the place mats don't have to match, but there should be some common thread that connects the look of the mats—color, style, or material.

I am a stickler about using cotton or linen napkins when entertaining formally or informally. They look and feel nicer to your guests and say, "Hey, you're important enough to me that I will do a load of laundry after you leave!"

For variety at an informal setting, napkins can be adorned with various flowers and placed in napkin rings. To add fine detail to any place setting, you can also use ribbon or tassels. Napkins should always lie flat in a simple fold for the most effective impression. Fancy folded napkins or bursts of napkins shooting from glasses distract from the setting as a whole. I find tying the napkin and placing it on a plate or to the left of the place setting is the most beautiful way to present the napkin.

Almost anything can be made into napkin rings using a glue gun and some creative flair. Handmade napkin rings add a wonderful personal touch to any party. I suggest keeping the design simple because you'll be making more than one, and when planning any party, time is surely an issue.

Here are eight napkin treatments you can easily make yourself:

1. Take loose faux jewels and glue them around a plain napkin ring. This is a wonderful way to add sparkle to a holiday table setting. You can use one-color jewels or a variety of colors, shapes, and sizes. Using crystal or diamond-like jewels is perfect for a special anniversary celebration or an April birthday party. (Diamonds are the birthstone for April.)

TUTERA TIP: Your local thrift store may be a source of secondhand linens as an alternative to buying new tablecloths or making them yourself.

2. Tying napkins with natural-colored raffia accented with horsetail bamboo is wonderful for a feng shui design. Adding a simple small orchid head will create a napkin treatment that is perfect for any tropical-themed party such as a luau or Polynesian night.

3. Look for napkin rings in thrift stores and at yard sales. This is a great way to create an eclectic mix-and-match look.

4. Napkins tied with ribbons that match the color scheme of the flowers or tablecloths give a simple, neat, color-coordinated look.

5. Think fun. Miniature silver Slinkys can be used to tie napkins for a children's party or for a futuristic theme. It's also a fun party favor for guests to take home.

6. Glow-in-the-dark necklaces wrapped around black napkins are fabulous for a children's party and add a funky glow to each table.

7. Make a collage out of pictures. For a birthday bash, use a variety of pictures of the guest of honor. Make several color laser copies on 11-by-17-inch card stock. Cut the card stock into strips 2 to 3 inches wide. Wrap the strips around napkin rings or sections of piping (available at any hardware store) and glue them on.

8. Take the heads of several red roses, miniature daisies, or mums and affix them to napkin rings with a glue gun. (Note: Use a cold glue gun rather than a hot one in order to protect the flowers.) This is a great look for a Valentine's Day celebration. You can also take small seashells or polished rocks and glue them to the napkin ring for a festive beach feel.

Runners offer a great opportunity to become creative. While the classic runner is a cloth running down the center of a rectangular table, I like to turn it into a long centerpiece. I've used beautiful antique tapestry runners, floated candles in long boxes of water, and even fashioned runners entirely from flowers. A runner can help define the dining area and create an interesting centerpiece without obstructing the views of your guests.

A few simple folds using beautiful cloth napkins add a unique touch to each place setting. In the top variation:

Step 1. Fold napkin into quarters with decorative corner facing down (top left).

Step 2. Fold top layer of decorative point halfway up front of napkin.

Step 3. Fold three bottom layers under.

Step 4. Fold both left and right tips under to make finished form (top right).

A second variation, above:

Step 1. Fold napkin into quarters with open points at top and folded point at bottom (bottom left).

Step 2. Fold top layer of top point halfway down front of napkin.

Step 3. Fold bottom corner under.

Step 4. Fold both left and right tips under to make finished form (bottom right).

CHINA, FLATWARE, AND GLASSWARE

While I approach every party intent on breaking the traditional rules, shattering the norm and taking ideas past ordinary boundaries. However, when it comes to planning and setting the perfect table, I am very traditional and generally stay within the rules. My choices for china, flatware, and glassware may be creative and colorful but would not be considered conservative or traditional in definition.

Whether you are entertaining at home or at a larger venue, the table setting is key to establishing the mood of the party. The setting should reflect the decor of the room and the style of service—formal or informal, buffet or sit-down—the number of courses being served, and the number of people eating. Once you have determined these details, you are ready to set your table or tables.

If you are entertaining at home, more than likely you will be the one placing each setting. Whether or not you own a full service for twenty-four people or two different sets of twelve, the idea is to make the table look as if there is a symmetrical flow. The average service usually has eighteen pieces, including six each of main, side, and sweet plates. The sweet plate is often used as a first-course plate. It is perfectly acceptable to use entirely different plates for dessert.

Mix-and-match china adds a unique touch to any place setting.

Dinnerware comes in a huge variety of colors, patterns, shapes, and sizes. You do not need a full set of china to entertain. Mix and match what you have, and if you need more plates, you can rent them from a party goods supplier or from your caterer if you have hired one.

Adding a fabulous charger plate can make a bold initial statement in any table setting. You can use the same service plates again and not leave your guests without a plate in front of them if you incorporate a charger plate. It is a visual benefit to any table setting. If you have enough plates, remove the charger plate with the serving of the first course.

When it comes to entertaining at home, clients frequently panic because of a shortage of cutlery. Check on your supply well in advance of the event to see what you have and what you will need to buy or rent. As long as guests have enough of each utensil when eating, the number of each you set initially doesn't really matter. There are three types of flatware: sterling silver, silverplate, and stainless steel. Some people have two sets, one in sterling for special occasions and one in stainless steel for everyday use. Silver and stainless steel come in a variety of patterns and designs. If you decide to invest in fine silver, try to select a classic and timeless design. It will last a lifetime and will work with virtually any place setting.

The basic five-piece setting consists of the following pieces, and utensils such as a fish knife, dessert fork, or demitasse spoon are optional.

TUTERA TIP: It may be necessary to spread out the various settings among several tables. The tables should have similar looks in which the centerpieces and place settings are coordinated.

- **Small fork:** first course, salad course, breakfast, lunch

- **Large fork:** lunch, main dinner course

- **Large spoon:** soup, dessert

- **Small spoon:** coffee, tea, dessert, fruit

- **Knife:** all meals

A traditional setting calls for forks to be set on the left-hand side of the place setting, and knives to the right. The spoon and fork for dessert may be placed either nearest to the place mat or, alternatively, at the top of each place setting. If placed at the top, the bowl of the spoon generally faces left and is placed above the fork, which faces right. If using a butter knife, place it horizontally at the top of the side plate. A side plate for bread and butter should be set on the left-hand side of the place setting.

Glass lends a certain grace and elegance to your table. The choice of stemware sizes, shapes, and colors is enormous. Crystal, handblown, and pressed glass are the three types of glassware. Traditionally, there is a purpose for every shape and size. It is customary to set a glass for each wine being served as well as a water glass, especially for more formal parties. Usually there are four glasses per person at a formal setting: one for white wine, served with the soup and fish course; one for red wine, to accompany the meat course; one for champagne, often served with dessert; and one for water. At less formal gatherings a single glass for wine and a water glass for each guest are fine. Taller highball glasses and short old-fashioned glasses are intended for use during the serving of cocktails. A beer mug, martini glass, and snifter are also intended for use during the serving of cocktails either before or after dinner.

The place setting is the center of each diner's attention, so it's important to put some thought into the look and placement of each element. Be sure to have salt and pepper shakers on the table. One set per two people is ideal although not essential. Other condiment dishes should be placed throughout the table as well, including dishes for butter, mustard, steak or fish sauce, and whatever else is appropriate for the meal you are serving. Bread plates are also a nice touch when setting a table.

If you are entertaining at a venue other than your home, consult the caterer (or whoever is responsible for the place settings) in advance to discuss the selection of dinnerware, flatware, and glassware available for your party. Ask to see how the table will be set on the day of your event.

Different glasses have very specific uses. From left to right, here are glasses for champagne, red wine, wine or water (all purpose), Martini, specialty drinks (such as Kir Royale, Manhattan, White Russian, etc.), Margaritas, liqueur, shot, high ball, and short Old Fashioned (or low ball).

65

TUTERA TIP: Tiny white Christmas lights can turn any room into a sparkling gem. You can use them in a variety of ways, including stringing them across the ceiling, around trees, or on a fireplace mantel. They're an inexpensive but elegant alternative to more elaborate lighting setups.

Changing the color of lighting throughout the course of a party will change the entire mood of the event.

CREATING ATMOSPHERE WITH LIGHTING

When it comes to planning a celebration, lighting is one of my real passions. It is an element that many people don't think about, and yet it is the most effective way to set a mood. Think about the sight sensation of a terrific lighting show. It leaves a lasting impression. Fantastic lighting always makes the most impressive impact, whether it's elaborate stage lighting or subdued, sexy candlelight. Perhaps because of my background in the theater, I always go for the most dramatic effect. But while I have spent tens of thousands of dollars creating lighting effects for events, I have also gotten away with using dimmers and candles to create equally impressive illumination.

Decide on the ambience and mood you want to create, and then customize your lighting accordingly. Make sure you select lighting colors that flatter skin tones. Pinks, ambers, and peaches are the best choices. Using these colors in your lighting design will give everyone a healthy, vivacious glow.

Place lighting strategically to hide flaws and highlight design elements in a room. Pin spotlights are an excellent way to illuminate florals because you can direct the light at a specific spot. It is best used when the beam of light comes from overhead or across the room.

If your budget allows for a more elaborate setup, I prefer to wash tables in a soft glow of light that highlights the whole area. Overall, this avoids a problem often incurred by the photographer, who must have ample lighting to capture the images of the event. If used properly, lighting will create a comfortable and cozy setting.

If you are having a large and more formal event with entertainment, lighting should be part of your budget. As discussed in the chapter on entertainment, some bands have lighting packages that are an additional cost. Make sure you are clear on what the entertainment is providing as far as lighting is concerned and whether there are any additional costs.

CANDLELIGHT

There is no prettier lighting hue than golden rich candlelight. I love to use candles for every type of event, large and small. Candlelight is

sexy, romantic, ethereal, peaceful, and calming in every way. It adds a feeling of intimacy even in a large venue. I try to use candles as often as possible, but there are some important things to consider before making that decision.

Candlelight does pose some safety hazards. As mentioned in chapter one, the use of open flames is restricted in a tented space. You can use battery-operated faux candles with the same effect. Mechanical candles are safer to use in all atmospheres. They are also a preference of mine if a waxy mess is a concern or if there are too many candles to manage and keep lit.

I use a variety of candles. Tall tapered candles are ideal for centerpieces in an elegant setting or candelabras. Votive candles are easily placed inside glass containers and are lovely for less formal events. Pillar candles are beautiful in almost any setting and come in many shapes, sizes, and colors.

TUTERA TIP: If you use open flame candles, make sure you keep the flame away from flowers, tablecloths, and other flammable materials.

67
Design Concepts

FLOWERS

Flowers bring life to any party through texture, color, and fragrance. Since the beginning of time, flowers have been used to reflect the individual lives of people. Floral designs have decorated celebrations for every occasion, and no doubt they will continue to do so for generations to come. I think of flowers as representing fine fabrics and materials I can work with to help create a living sculpture. Floral design has been an integral part of my business, and like a woodworker artist, I continue to perfect this aspect of my craft. Floral design was the basis for the formation of my company, and it remains a signature element for any event I plan, produce, or coordinate. I would love to share every gem of information in my head about flowers and floral designing, but that would be an entire book in itself. Instead, I hope you'll take away from this section a better understanding of how to work with a professional, whether that person is from your local flower shop or is a more sophisticated designer, and not be intimidated in the process. Granted, not everyone has the desire to understand the finer aspects of botany or horticulture, but that is why there are experts you can turn to for advice. The basics are the same regardless of how large your needs are when it comes to flowers and floral arrangements. There are six main areas to be considered when it comes to the floral design of an event: design types, size, color, texture, fragrance, and containers.

There are many possibilities when it comes to deciding where flowers should be placed for any event. You have to decide on the locations that are best for you depending on the event and your budget. The most common areas I design arrangements for are as follows:

Entry	Ceiling treatments
Escort card tables	Cake table
Bathrooms	Serving trays
Cocktail tables	Napkin treatments
Buffet tables	Bridal bouquets
Bars	Boutonnieres
Guest tables	Additional bridal party personal flowers and corsages
Dessert tables	
Stage treatments	

DESIGN TYPES

Like a fabulous work of art, each creation by a florist or designer is a one-of-a-kind original. Just as an interior designer chooses specific artwork for a space, a floral designer fashions each arrangement to work within the space and to enhance the appearance of your particular event. Many times, flowers are the only element of design used as decoration for a party. They become even more important when they serve this double purpose because they add color and life to the space and are the most visible element besides the room itself.

Adding a light mist of water with a spray bottle to the flowers prior to the start of a party adds a wonderful fresh look to the arrangement. Be careful not to overmist the flowers since it can create moisture on the tablecloths and glassware.

A professional designer instinctively knows how to serve both needs. If you don't like a particular type of flower, simply tell your florist or designer in advance. Once you set the boundaries, he or she can create wonderful arrangements within them. Additionally, when used to maximum potential, flowers can bring another level of ambience and magic to a room, whether it be in a home, a tent, or anywhere else. Flowers are a reflection of life, love, and happiness; they are Mother Nature at her most elegant expression.

Floral designs have an impact on the final visual appearance. The first thing I ask a client in order to find the appropriate design is the type of look he or she is hoping to achieve. The kinds of flowers used, the size of each variety, and the design approach vary greatly from party to party. Each historical period also influences floral designs, and each generation's views reflect the way people live in the world. As a result, my floral designs usually fall into three main categories: contemporary, traditional, and classical.

CONTEMPORARY These are my specialty. They always have strong, sleek lines, usually consisting of vertical stemmed florals. Although usually minimalistic, these designs have a sturdy look with the least amount of placement. Asian-influenced designs are quite popular in contemporary arrangements because they are open and flowing. There is always a symmetrical line in Asian designs that gives the cleanest, purest, and usually simplest look to the arrangement.

TRADITIONAL The baroque influence is most apparent in traditional designs. Roses are frequently selected to create a pavé look that consists of blocks of colors used together to fashion an overall design. Traditional designs are the most complex to prepare because, while they look less arranged than other types of designs, each stem is carefully placed.

CLASSICAL To me, classical designs look and feel Victorian in appearance. They are very full and abundant designs, bursting with color and variety. They have a lot of opulence, a feminine influence, and several layers of depth, consisting of short-, medium-, and long-stemmed flowers. Together, these layers make for an almost three-dimensional look to each arrangement. Classical arrangements are like Impressionist paintings. There is never an empty space, and the appearance is as beautiful close up as it is from afar.

SIZE

Arrangements do not need to be enormous to be grand, nor do they need to be elaborate to make a lasting impression. Designs vary according to individual needs and budget. Consider the size of the space in which your party is taking place. Floral arrangements should never be bigger than a space can hold; they become cumbersome and overwhelming for everyone.

One of my best design secrets is combining large arrangements with smaller ones to give a wavelike appearance to table centerpieces. Alternating tables of large centerpieces with tables of smaller, lower ones achieves this effect and creates a more customized look in a generally sterile-looking room.

COLOR

Color is one of the most important elements in flower arranging. Color may be the only thing some of your guests remember about the arrangements. Many people have no idea what kinds of flowers are used in arrangements, but everyone remembers a vibrant burst of bright and bold color. Think back to your early school days when you learned about Sir Isaac Newton's scientific theory that color is a property of light. By passing white light through a prism, he caused the light to separate into a rainbow of colors because of the varying wavelengths. Apply this theory to your planning process when making your floral selections. Have you ever put on a pair of black pants that ended up looking brown in the light? Keep the environment of your event in mind when selecting your flowers. The lighting can dramatically affect the color perceived.

Since color creates a mood or setting for any event, I have defined two groups of colors I work with when designing arrangements with clients, warm colors and cool colors. Warm colors are red, orange, and yellow. Cool colors are blue, green, and purple.

Warm colors are associated with warm things, such as the sun, fire, and heat. They are joyful full-of-life colors that evoke cheerful feelings. Cool colors represent cool things such as grass, water, and ice. They are restful, peaceful, and soothing to the eye. Blending

OPPOSITE The arrangements illustrate the concepts (from top to bottom) of contemporary, traditional, and classical floral design.

BELOW A small bouquet of delicate flowers in a frosted crystal vase adds a marvelous element to each place setting and makes a wonderful favor for each of your guests.

71

Design Concepts

*M*ONEY-SAVING TIPS FOR FLORAL DESIGNS

- Try to reuse flowers later in the party. Bridal bouquets look wonderful as an embellishment on the cake table or on the bride and groom's table.

- For a more casual design, seasonal flowering plants placed in the center of each guest table can create a warm garden setting. Be sure to embellish the plants with a wonderful basket container, moss, ivy, and ribbons for a complete look.

- Simple arrangements are sometimes the least costly and still look amazing. A bouquet of tulips gathered and placed in a simple and elegant glass container is a lovely centerpiece for a luncheon, baby shower, or small dinner party at home.

- At the end of your party, you might want to allow your guests to take home the flower arrangements as a gift, or you can contact a local hospital or nursing home and donate the flowers to patients.

Combining different types of flowers adds texture to the look of a bouquet. In this case, using large-headed flowers with small ones successfully creates texture and drama.

warm and cool colors can create a visual balance in most arrangements and increase their depth, making them more interesting looking.

The use of color evokes a subconscious emotional response. Everyone has a favorite color, and it is easy to include that color in your arrangements. Red and green instantly bring to mind holiday spirits. Red, pink, and white roses easily identify Valentine's Day or being in love. Pastel colors are common for springtime, whereas orange, yellow, brown, and red are thought of as autumn colors. The effect of color may be subconscious, but it is almost always powerful.

TEXTURE

Texture refers to the surface characteristics of any object. It is the tactile exterior quality of an entity, especially when it comes to floral designs. Although you might not actually feel the texture of a floral composition, our memory provides a sensory reaction. Visual texture arouses tactile sensation. A good example of this is the texture of clouds. We think of clouds as being soft and fluffy, like cotton. But in reality clouds are a mass of tiny water droplets or suspended ice crystals. We often think of textures as being rough or smooth, shiny or dull, coarse or fine. When it comes to floral arrangements, texture is important in the selection of every material you use, from the flowers to the containers. Every flower has texture. Some are soft in appearance, while others are more rigid. In floral designs, texture is heightened by the juxtaposition of varied and opposite surfaces. You'll want to select a variety of surfaces and textures for the greatest depth and impact. Using a combination of different types of flowers and greenery, such as tree branches or stems of flowering branches, is the best way to create uniqueness and texture in your designs. Combining various sizes and varieties of flowers in different kinds of containers will maximize the texture your guests perceive in each arrangement.

FRAGRANCE

Fragrance was once regarded as the single most important aspect of flowers because it was believed that the odor would ward off disease. Fragrance is often overlooked as an element of floral designing, and yet the additional sensory dimension only heightens the pleasure and awareness of any environment. Smell can be an effective method for remembering a specific moment in time such as a joyous celebration. It can transport us back in time.

I never take the smell of flowers for granted, and I work with them every day. Many of my clients would be disappointed in an arrangement, no matter how beautiful, if it didn't pack a fragrant pungent punch. Certain scents are personal favorites, such as gardenia, lily of the valley, and tuberose.

Strong fragrances should be avoided in designs that are intended for small spaces. They can become overwhelming. Allergies to certain fragrances are another issue to consider when choosing flowers. The scent of flowers and foliage varies from sweet and delicate to spicy and bold. Try to incorporate fragrances into your selection of flowers if possible. Your guests will be most impressed.

The following flowers have a more potent fragrance, which should be kept in mind when dealing with allergies or a smaller enclosed area: hyacinths, freesia, gardenias, lilies, paperwhites, stock, and tuberoses. Remember, too, that having overly fragrant flowers on a dining table can affect the taste of the food.

TUTERA TIP: Fragrance is not limited to flowers. Herbs such as rosemary and mint add fragrance and are relatively inexpensive to use. Fruits, such as lemons, limes, apples, and oranges, are also an easy and inexpensive way to add fresh fragrance. Fresh wheat grass, which I use often in my designs, is also a popular choice because it adds an outdoorsy aroma.

CONTAINERS

All floral arrangements are designed to be placed in a holding container, a vase, urn, bucket, bowl, or other type of vessel. The container is the foundation of the floral composition and should never be inferior to the arrangement itself. There are as many containers to choose from as there are flowers, and they come in a wide variety of shapes, sizes, styles, materials, and prices. The container you choose depends on your choice of flowers and where the arrangement is being placed. The container needs to be compatible with the design and setting, both visually and physically.

Selecting the proper size and shape of the container is essential for creating unified designs. Choose a container that complements the overall design concept for your event. Baroque containers do not flow with a contemporary theme. Likewise, a black deco container may look out of place at a bridal shower done in pastel colors. Keeping the container in proper proportion to the arrangement will give the best overall effect. Flowers that are too large for the container are an accident waiting to happen.

Containers come in many different materials, including glass, plastic, wicker, ceramic, brass, and stainless steel. I generally use glass and stainless steel containers for my designs. As long as the container is visually appealing and adds a certain decorative appeal, it is a good choice regardless of the material.

TUTERA TIP: Using bold, vibrant colors in your flowers and using a monochromatic approach to the design will give the impression that you spent more money on the arrangements because the contrast and impact are more dramatic and visually appealing.

FLOWER VARIETIES

Don't insist on using flowers that are not in season. You can save a lot of money by using flowers that are available and in season when making your selection. Also many wonderful flowers available year-round can work just as well as seasonal flowers.

Don't be afraid to go for the unexpected! An exotic flower can still have a romantic look. Have fun and experiment. A party is a perfect reason to go for the biggest impact.

SPRING	SUMMER	FALL	WINTER	YEAR-ROUND
Anemone	Aster	Aster	Amaryllis	Alstromeria
Apple blossom	Bells of Ireland	Bittersweet	Camellia	Bachelor button
Cherry blossom	Calla lily	Celosia	Daffodil	Carnation
Daffodil	Dahlia	Chinese lantern	Ginestra	Daisy
Freesia	Fuchsia	Chrysanthemum	Hyacinth	Delphinium
Iris	Geranium	Dahlia	Mimosa	Fern
Lilac	Gladiola	Fuchsia	Paperwhite narcissus	Gardenia
Lily of the valley	Honeysuckle	Hydrangea	Star-of-Bethlehem	Ivy
Peony	Hydrangea	Marigold	Tulip	Lily
Quince	Orange blossom	Montbretia		Orchid
Sweet pea	Zinnia	Zinnia		Rose
Tulip				Stephanotis
Violet				

4 | Food, Drinks, and Caterers

Food is one of the most memorable elements of any gathering, and the way that it is served sets the tempo for the party. When selecting a menu, try to recall some of your favorite dining memories. What are some of the most inspired appetizers or main courses that come to mind? Don't try to impress your guests with complicated, abundant meals filled with exotic and extreme flavors and tastes. Think about the foods you like to eat and use that as a barometer when selecting the courses. Despite the grandest fears, guests rarely leave a party feeling hungry. Keeping the choices simple will guarantee a good meal and a good time for everyone, including yourself. The night of the party is not the time to get daring and try foods you have never eaten or considered. Save that idea for another night. Whether you're working with a caterer or preparing the food yourself, a well-planned meal cooked and served on a set timetable is the best way to tackle this sometimes daunting duty.

While speaking with several of the caterers I use around the country, I found that the trends in catering vary depending on where you live. While the West Coast used to concentrate on serving lighter fare, there seems to be a push toward comfort foods and getting back to the basics. The East Coast seems to be lightening things up a bit, keeping menu selections quite eclectic and healthy. Asian foods are a popular choice for the parties that I'm planning up and down the east-

When serving buffet style, it is as important for the dishes to be easily accessible as it is for the food to be displayed beautifully.

77

ern seaboard. I am often asked to provide menus that are influenced by a specific ethnicity. These work well in all areas of the country because they allow your guests to experience something new, almost like traveling to a different land. Of course, like all trends, food selection changes with the seasons. And don't think I'm forgetting all of you who live in between the coasts. Colleagues of mine tell me that the trends in these regions follow the coasts very closely.

Trust your caterer to recommend his or her best dishes. Take the chef's suggestions. There has to be a trust factor such as the one you have with your doctor. Oftentimes a client will want something that is great in a restaurant but terrible to serve in large quantities. We're serving a lot of comfort foods and less nouvelle cuisine. People are asking for veal and lamb, which are great served at large functions.

BARBARA BRASS
WOLFGANG PUCK CATERING AND SPECIAL EVENTS
BEVERLY HILLS, CA

RIGHT *Keep hors d'oeuvres small, in bite-size portions, for any cocktail party.*

OPPOSITE *Spectacular presentation is a great way to impress guests—but be sure the food tastes as good as it looks.*

A Passion for Parties

Nothing is more dazzling at the height of the summer than a fresh tomato salad.

In the summer we use a lot of heirloom tomatoes, lobster, shrimp, lump crabmeat, and corn—foods that are readily available, abundant, and in season. In the winter people lean toward heartier, more rugged dishes: upscale casseroles served in individual china dishes, seafood ragout, and game cassoulet with beans and sausage served with caramelized acorn squash.

ALISON AWERBUCH
ABIGAIL KIRSCH CULINARY
PRODUCTIONS
TARRYTOWN, NY

TYPES OF FOOD

In general I prefer food that is light both in appearance and in fare. Big, heavy, creamy meals tend to make guests feel tired and lethargic, which keeps the party tempo turned way down. Think about your guest list when deciding on your menu. Do you have health-conscious guests who watch their fat and calorie intake, or do you have meat and potato eaters? Does your party plan call for an ethnic flavor in the food you serve, a kosher meal, or some other theme such as Mexican? Many people these days are on a restricted diet due to allergies, weight problems, or religious or health restrictions, so trying to come up with one menu to please them all can be a real challenge. Don't let those restrictions stand in the way of planning a delicious, flavorful meal, but keep the limitations in mind when deciding on the menu and be certain to offer a variety of options to please even the most finicky guests.

SERVICE STYLE

Clients often get carried away with the idea of planning elaborate multicourse meals. I explain to them that they're dealing with a very limited window of time, and they must consider what other element of the party will suffer as a result of a long meal service. Extended meals might mean less dancing, less revelry, and less celebrating. The overall ambience becomes staid, and for some events that is perfectly fine, but usually it is not as much fun. Ask yourself why you're celebrating and then decide how much time you want to devote to eating. Keeping a flow of motion throughout an event is a key element in keeping spirits high in any room. You can serve elaborate food, but I shy away from traditional service such as formal French service, which, while quite elegant, really locks your guests into one seat for a very long period of time. I often suggest serving only the first course and following it with buffet service around the room. This allows guests to get up and move at their own pace and eat as much or as little as they want, and when they want.

SELECTING A CATERER

When planning a party, you have the options of hiring a caterer, carrying out from a restaurant, or preparing the meal yourself. When choosing to work with a caterer, keep in mind that some caterers are known for serving a particular type of cuisine. Learn what your caterer does best and take advantage of that special talent. Some specialize in large parties, some are ideal for intimate gatherings, and others are equipped to do only commercial catering.

It is important to get recommendations from friends and family who have hosted an event and were very pleased with their caterer's services. Word of mouth is the best way to learn about the better caterers. You can also check with the National Caterers Association for references (www.ncacater.org). Make sure your caterer is licensed, certified, and insured.

Decide on your food budget ahead of time and work with your caterer to select the kinds of food that fit within that budget. Find out what is included in the caterer's price. Does the estimate include serving pieces? Buffet decor? Make sure you are not being billed for something twice, such as centerpieces. If your florist is providing them, your caterer doesn't need to. If your caterer is creative and experienced, an exciting and delectable menu can be accomplished on any budget. A professional caterer will provide you with a formal proposal that itemizes the cost per person, the exact menu, and the agreed-upon services and supplies to be provided.

If your event calls for a particular cuisine, try to find a restaurant or caterer that specializes in preparing that type of food. You'll be hard-pressed to find a caterer that prepares Indian food better than an authentic Indian restaurant; for Japanese food, especially sushi, your best bet is a quality Japanese restaurant. Many established restaurants are happy to work with you to prepare meals of any size. Make

TUTERA TIP: Work with vendors who are in business to take care of you. Sometimes the personality of a vendor can become very high maintenance, and you might find that you're spending more time making sure your vendor is happy than vice versa.

Your caterer only knows what you tell him or her. It's important to keep your caterer abreast of the number of people you expect. If you are going to have more or less than the number of guests agreed upon, it affects every vendor you're working with. It might mean setting three more tables of ten or reducing your place settings by that same amount. If you add tables, you must also add centerpieces, rent more place settings, add more food, liquor, and staff, etc. When your numbers grow, it affects every entity involved in the event. Allowing an extra cushion in your budget for these unexpected expenses will help eliminate last-minute stress and panic. There are always miscellaneous expenses that people forget about or are not expecting.

BARBARA BRASS
WOLFGANG PUCK CATERING AND SPECIAL EVENTS
BEVERLY HILLS, CA

sure they have had experience with off-site catering if they are going to prepare the food outside of the restaurant.

Seasonal menus for events are becoming all the rage. There is no better way to welcome a particular holiday than enjoying a food that simulates the flavor and spirit of that holiday. Each season has aromas, tastes, and colors that are easily associated and identified with that particular time of year. Spring and summer are filled with lighter tastes and foods, while fall and winter tend to be a little richer and bolder in flavor and cuisine. According to several caterers I work with, there is a trend toward certain foods during the different seasons of the year.

Once you've decided on a caterer, have him or her come to your home to do a site inspection. If you are renting a facility that requires you to bring in an outside caterer, make arrangements for him or her to visit. Your caterer should see the space he or she will be working in and become familiar with the limitations and accommoda-

The freshest ingredients, simple presentation, and impeccable service will never go out of style.

DAVID CASTLE
SONNIER & CASTLE
CATERING
NEW YORK, NY

82

tions. Show the caterer where everything is in advance so you will not be bothered by simple requests during the event, such as where the garbage is supposed to go. If you are entertaining in a space that does not have a kitchen, such as a tent, make sure your caterer has had sufficient experience working in those conditions. Some caterers specialize in off-site catering.

A caterer often provides many more services than just food preparation, such as your entire wait staff, bartenders, cleaning crew, and kitchen staff. The general rule for wait staff is 1.5 waiters per table. Some caterers also offer additional staffing, including coat check personnel and bathroom attendants.

Discuss with your caterer a uniform look for all personnel at your event. I suggest to my clients that whenever possible, they avoid having staff dressed in all black attire. It can confuse your guests, especially at a formal event when everyone is dressed primarily in all black. Long white aprons are a nice way to differentiate the staff from guests, and you'll avoid that embarrassing moment of accidentally asking the father of the bride for a gin and tonic! At less formal events I suggest a uniform look for staff such as black pants and a white shirt or three-quarter-length Asian-inspired jackets. A festive Hawaiian shirt or hula skirt is fun for a beach party, backyard barbecue, or Polynesian fete. And if you're hosting something a little more risqué, leather and lace is a fine substitute for the staff.

SERVICE MATTERS

Whether hosting a formal gathering or an intimate get-together, service is the main ingredient to hosting a quality affair. The timing of service is essential to keeping a certain flow. If the food is served late or at inappropriate times when it comes to the rest of the events happening, it can throw your entire party off schedule and create a major disruption. Discuss your service needs in advance with the caterer and put them in writing.

Your caterer must have ample time to hire the best people. You'll want to make sure to ask your caterer about hiring experienced staff. Having a bowl of soup served in a guest's lap or a piece of chicken accidentally fall into Aunt Sophie's pocketbook takes away

Be sure passed hors d'oeuvres are evenly spaced on the tray so that guests can easily pick them up.

TUTERA TIP: Leftover food from your event can be donated to a local homeless shelter or soup kitchen at no cost to you. Local charities will help make arrangements to pick up the food and deliver it to those in need.

from the fun. There are plenty of companies that require their staff to have extensive backgrounds in food service.

Keep in mind that most caterers specify prices based on the inclusion of minimum staff to accommodate your party. Additional hired staff is likely to become an additional cost to you, so be very clear to ask your caterer about the total fees. An event that is well catered is less stress and aggravation for you. Work with the pros that handle these types of parties every week. They'll know the ins and outs of catering, virtually guaranteeing a successful and hectic-free gathering for everyone.

One final thought on service: It is important to know about tipping your staff. The general rule is to tip at least 15 percent of the actual food costs. It is customary to tip the person in charge of the catering, who will then split the tip among the key workers. If your event is at a hotel, tip the catering manager. If you are working with an outside caterer, tip the person you have worked with most closely. If you are using only personnel, tip each server the same amount. If you are working with a planner, have that person coordinate the disbursements on your behalf.

> Raw bars with oysters and clams on the half shell are really popular. We'll do a variety of four or five different types of oysters, clams, shrimp, and stone crab claws when in season. Sushi bars are also very popular. Martini bars and vodka and caviar bars never go out of style. A shot glass of chilled soup is a nice passed hors d'oeuvre, as is lobster flan baked in an eggshell. For entrées we're serving a lot of rack of lamb and lobster.
>
> ALISON AWERBUCH
> ABIGAIL KIRSCH CULINARY PRODUCTIONS
> TARRYTOWN, NY

COOKING AT HOME

My philosophy about food at a party is the same whether you have it catered or prepare the meal yourself: Keep it simple! Try to plan a menu that can be prepared in advance. As a host you should not spend your entire time in the kitchen. Planning a menu that allows you time to enjoy your party is the real secret to a successful party in which you prepare the food yourself.

When your guest list starts to creep above twenty people, every aspect of the food and service becomes unmanageable. Think about creating a menu that consists of foods you can make in large portions, such as pasta, flank steak, chicken, turkey, salads, soups, and simple vegetables. Family-style dining is always fun and is fairly hassle-free once the food is served.

You really cannot find a restaurant or hotel as intimate and welcoming as your own home.

For more formal dinner parties, the menu can still be simple, but the presentation can look elegant. Sometimes how food is served is as important as what is being served. (In fact, this is true whether you're cooking at home or catering a large event.) When cooking at home, your kitchen will be in full swing. This sometimes means a drastic rise in temperature throughout the home. It also means that your home will be chock-full of aromatic sensations that, it is hoped, will entice and not disgust your guests. On the day of the event, the heat from the kitchen can wilt center-pieces, make a soufflé fall, and melt the makeup right off that pretty little face.

Accent a Tuscan buffet with miniature terracotta pots filled with tea lights.

TUTERA TIP: If you decide to prepare the food for your party yourself, you may still want to consider hiring a staff to help serve and clean. This relieves you of various tasks and helps you to be a gracious host. You can find service staff by asking for recommendations from friends or looking under "Party Help," "Party Supplies," or "Employment Contractors" in your local yellow pages.

PARTY RENTALS

You can rent almost anything you need for a party these days. Tables, chairs, china, silverware, and glassware are all available from party rental services. It used to be that you could choose only between basic white china or white china with a gold rim when renting. Nowadays the choices are as varied as your guest list. You can get creative and match your chairs to your place settings or the stemware to your linens. Most caterers have wonderful relationships with rental companies, and they will be happy to put you in touch directly or provide the service themselves.

      When I work with a client, I like to work directly with the rental supplier to try to match the look of the party with the proper accoutrements. If the party has a theme, I look for plates and linens to complement the theme. Rental services have made throwing a theme party easier than ever. Be aware, though, that party rentals can consume a large portion of your event budget. If that is a concern, try to use what you have and then rent an eclectic mix of items to finish the look.

BAR POSITION

A self-service vodka and caviar tray for a cocktail party.

When setting up any room for a party, the bar is usually the most densely populated area. Where you set up the bar will greatly impact the traffic flow. Pick a location that is unencumbered and open. If your space allows for more than one bar, all the better! Ideally, you want to keep things moving along. Long lines create unnecessary traffic jams, and, frankly, you know how irritable some people can get when they *need* that next drink!

BEVERAGE SELECTION

I suggest to my clients that a "specialty bar" be set up. It becomes a center of attention in any room but also allows guests to get a drink quickly and easily. For example, I may set up a martini bar that serves several different types of martinis. A margarita bar is another option. One idea for a specialty bar that I wouldn't suggest comes from one

I prefer a self-service bar when entertaining at home in small groups. Guests are happy to help themselves, and I find that it often serves as a way for people to get to know each other.

Twisted bamboo skewers offer a unique substitute for the rather ordinary cocktail pick.

of my colleagues. He had a client who insisted on a martini bar that featured oyster shooters—a shot of vodka with a fresh raw oyster at the bottom. This caterer friend of mine reluctantly obliged his client's request but included in his contract that he would not clean up the mess if anyone got sick. Yuck!

A WELL-STOCKED BAR

You never know who may drop by unexpectedly, so it's always a good idea to keep your bar at home stocked with the bare essentials. Hosting a party is a great excuse to get your bar up to date and ready for any occasion. A properly stocked bar should consist of the following items at a minimum. Of course, everyone has different tastes about the brands they prefer, so select the ones that you like best.

MIXERS Tonic, seltzer, club soda, lime juice, dry and sweet vermouth, margarita and sour mixes

JUICES Orange, tomato, cranberry, grapefruit, pineapple

GARNISHES Lemons, limes, olives, onions, margarita salt, bitters

LIQUOR Vodka, gin, rum, scotch, rye, tequila

LIQUEUR Brandy, Cointreau, Grand Marnier, Triple Sec

WINE AND CHAMPAGNE White wine, such as chardonnay, pinot grigio, and sauvignon blanc; red wine, such as merlot and cabernet; zinfandel; champagne and sparkling wines

OTHER ESSENTIALS Sodas (cola, diet cola, ginger ale, 7UP); nonalcoholic beer; beer and light beer, preferably bottled; bottled water, sparkling and flat

BARWARE Corkscrew, bottle opener, ice bucket and tongs, sharp knife, cutting board, swizzle sticks, straws, jigger, shot glass, martini shaker, pitcher, blender, cocktail napkins, coasters, toothpicks

The following are the most popular martinis I serve at events. You can experiment with the recipes. Have fun making these for your next swanky affair!

MARTINI CLASSICS

Dirty Martini

3 parts vodka
1 part olive juice
1 part extra dry vermouth

Mix all ingredients with ice and strain into a martini glass. Garnish with 3 olives. Best served cold.

Elegant Martini

6 parts gin
2 parts dry vermouth
1 part Grand Marnier orange liqueur

Stir the gin, vermouth, and half the Grand Marnier with ice. Strain or serve with ice. Float the remaining Grand Marnier on top.

TRENDY MARTINIS

Cosmo Martini

4 parts vodka
1 part Cointreau orange liqueur
1 part cranberry juice
1 splash club soda
1 lime twist

Pour vodka, Cointreau, and cranberry juice over ice and shake well. Strain into a glass and splash with club soda. Rub the rim of the glass with the lime and then place the lime in the glass.

Lemon Drop Martini

4 parts vodka
1 part frozen lemonade concentrate
1 lemon twist

Pour ingredients over ice and shake well to mix. Pour or strain into a glass. Garnish with the lemon twist. (There is real pucker appeal to this, but it is refreshing on a hot night.)

DESSERT MARTINIS

After-Eight Martini

2 parts vodka
2 parts white crème de cacao
1 part crème de menthe

Shake all the ingredients in a shaker; serve over ice, with a cherry if desired. (This is not nearly as good served without ice.)

Chocolate Martini

2 parts vodka
1 part white crème de cacao
1 splash dry vermouth
1 lemon twist
Dusting of cocoa powder

Moisten the edge of a glass with the lemon twist and dip into a flat plate of cocoa powder to rim the edge. Pour liquid ingredients into a shaker with ice and shake well. Strain into the chilled martini glass.

Appletini

2 parts vodka
1 part Triple Sec
1 part Apple Pucker apple sour

Shake all ingredients with ice and strain into a chilled glass.

TUTERA TIP: If your group requires more than the average amounts of alcohol given in the table below, contact Betty Ford for a group discount.

It is usually best to keep the bar simple so that service for a large number of guests can be efficient. Remember that a party bar is set up to serve guests with ease and graciousness. It is not a public bar, so requests for Mai Tais, sloe gin fizzes, and Brandy Alexanders need not be anticipated. It is very difficult to dictate the stocking of a bar, since tastes vary, but generally a wine and liquor bar for a four- to six-hour period should contain the following:

The following are recommended items and amounts for parties of 50, 100, 200, and 350 guests.

NUMBER OF GUESTS	50	100	200*	350
LIQUOR (Liters)				
Bourbon	1	2	6	6
Campari	1	2	4	6
Dry Vermouth	1	2	4	6
Gin (more in summer)	2	4	8	12
Rum	1	2	6	6
Rye	1	2	4	6
Scotch (more in winter)	4	6	12	16
Sweet Vermouth	1	2	4	6
Tequila	1	3	6	10
Vodka	4	6	20	24
WINE (750 mL)				
Red wine (more in winter)	8	8	60**	9
White wine (more in summer)	12	16	84**	12
CHAMPAGNE (750 mL)				
(For toast only)	8	12	28	48
(At the bar only)	8	16	36	56
BEER (Cases)				
Light	1	2	3	5
Imported	1	2	3	5

NUMBER OF GUESTS	50	100	200*	350
SODA (Cases)				
Cola	1½	2	4	8
Diet cola	1½	1½	3	6
Ginger ale	½	1	2	4
Seltzer	1	3	4	6
7UP	½	1	2	4
Tonic	½	1	2	4
Mineral water	½	1	3	5
JUICE (Gallons)				
Cranberry	1	1½	3	6
Grapefruit	1	1	2	3
Orange	1½	2	3	5
Tomato	½	4	5	8
MISCELLANEOUS (Cases)†				
Brandy or Cognac	1	2	4	5
Dubonnet	1	2	4	5

* Standard bar for an evening party; allow for 2 double bars to be set up.

** For bar only. If wine is to be poured at the tables, allow an additional 12 bottles of red and 30 bottles of white.

† Not really necessary unless you know some guests may request them. Cordials require that you rent another type of glass.

Food, Drinks, and Caterers

5 | Entertainment

Entertainment is the heartbeat of any large party. From the moment guests arrive, music and entertainment underscore everything that's happening around them. Entertainment can mean music—a disc jockey or live band—a floor show, magicians, psychics, dancers, music or presentation videos, and the list goes on and on. While some event planners think music can be a distraction, to me it is an essential element to any gathering, large or small. Music can create an ambience that is thrilling, dramatic, romantic, fun, festive, or subdued. As an event planner I think that you have to capture your guests' attentions within the first two minutes of their arrival or you lose them. If I don't create the perfect setting from the start, I feel as though I'm playing catch-up for the rest of the event. Music is a sure-fire way to excite your guests.

MUSICAL STYLE GUIDE

Selecting the entertainment for your event is a very personal task. It should really be a reflection of who you are as the host and what pleases you. Keeping that in mind, if your tastes run a little eccentric and you know that the majority of your guests don't share your enthusiasm for the kind of music you prefer, make the decision to balance

TUTERA TIP: Prepackaged cocktail music is available on specialty CDs and tapes. They contain a variety of artists who are ideal for such a gathering.

your tastes with more mainstream selections to keep the mood even-keeled throughout the party. There is nothing worse than suffering through several music selections that no one recognizes, can't dance to, can barely understand the words to, and are downright irritating! (Been there, done that!) When I discuss entertainment options with my clients, I spend a great deal of time finding out what types of music they listen to at home and in the car; what they dance to and relax to; what they like when having dinner, and even when making love. (I really don't need to know the last one, but I'm just plain nosy!) Most of my clients are surprised when they discover that they're not sure what they like, and it usually becomes a homework assignment. Over the years I have accumulated an extensive list of songs that are popular for specific events, plus a variety of artists to consider when planning entertainment. Here are some to contemplate:

When guests are over, always try to provide some sort of background music, whether live or electronic.

- For a formal affair—that is, for a cocktail reception, dinner music, or romantic setting—there's Cole Porter, Stephen Sondheim, Duke Ellington, Frank Sinatra, Glenn Miller, Nat King Cole, Ella Fitzgerald, Billie Holiday, George Gershwin, and Count Basie.
  Classical and chamber music includes Bach, Handel, Mozart, and Vivaldi.

- Dance music—which is fitting for between-meal courses and post-dinner dancing—may include Motown, R&B, disco, and seventies classics, Top 40, big band, and swing music, such as the Tommy Dorsey, Benny Goodman, and Glenn Miller orchestras.

- Ethnic music is best used in connection with a religious celebration or a theme party and can include these varieties: Israeli folk selections, Caribbean steel drums, reggae, Irish folk and popular types, accordion, opera, mariachi, salsa, polkas, and Greek festival pieces.

- Romantic music can be played on any occasion for parties from two to two hundred. Favorites include Barbra Streisand, Céline Dion, Frank Sinatra, Billy Joel, Harry Connick Jr., Natalie Cole, Luther Vandross, Barry White, Enigma, Aria, Olive, and Sting.

- Broadway favorites are always great during cocktails and after dinner. They are a real show stopper with a piano bar. They can be from *Cats, Les Misérables, West Side Story, Phantom of the Opera,* and *Funny Girl,* and all Sondheim and Gershwin show tunes are superb.

Once my client reviews these lists, we discuss their preferences, and I am able to discern the most suitable choices for their upcoming event. Sometimes, though, clients have a definite opinion on the kind of entertainment they want. Frequently a client tells me about a "great" band he heard on vacation or in a local bar. He'll spend fifteen minutes convincing me that this is the band they want for their wedding. I hate to be a killjoy, but inevitably I have to explain that while they may have enjoyed that band on that occasion, they are not the ideal band for this occasion. Although I try to avoid using traditional entertainment for any kind of party, there is one important point: bands and disc jockeys that specialize in performing at parties are usually the best choice for entertainment regardless of event. The entertainment must adhere to a time line that is predetermined to keep a party moving, and entertainers who specialize in parties are more familiar with this kind of formula than those who play the bar and club circuit. That's not to say that you can't use the less experienced entertainers, but more preplanning would be necessary to assure the pace of the evening and time schedule. The choices of entertainment are limitless; unfortunately, your budget is probably not. The following may help you decide what is best for your needs.

HIRING A DISC JOCKEY

Disc jockeys (DJs) are an excellent choice for large and small parties. Many of my clients prefer working with a DJ because the play list can be customized to suit their wishes. Although DJs used to be associated with parties for younger crowds, that is no longer the case. Clients of all ages like to work with DJs rather than a band because they interact with the crowd more. They get people up and dancing if the mood is too staid. They're also very good at intermingling the various generations that otherwise wouldn't mix. A good DJ is the conductor of energy in any room and knows when it's time to heat things up or slow things down. A DJ is generally less expensive than a band, but frequently the decision is not based on money but on the spirit of the event. The average cost of a five-hour event, which includes setting up and breaking down the equipment, can range from $750 to $3,000. Like everything else I've mentioned, you can find a good DJ by obtaining referrals from friends or family members, or by selecting one you enjoyed as a guest at another event.

The following are suggestions about what to do if you want to hire a disc jockey for your event:

1. To find the best DJs in your area, contact local entertainment companies that specialize in providing entertainers for parties.

2. Ask for a list of the types of parties the DJ has worked.

3. Meet the DJ to learn about his or her personality and style. Discuss your wishes and needs for your particular party, including the DJ's wardrobe for the event. Exchange ideas and possibilities in order to ascertain the DJ's experience.

4. Ask to see the DJ in action. If at all possible, arrange to preview his or her performance. Many professional DJs have a demonstration videotape that you can view in lieu of attending another client's event.

5. Plan your play list in advance to be certain the DJ has the selections you want. It is not unusual for a DJ to get a request for Tom Jones or the best of Lawrence Welk, so in order to keep everyone happy, discuss these items before the fete.

6. An experienced DJ comes with all his or her own equipment, which usually includes props he or she may need, all music selections, speakers and sound system, and an announcer's microphone.

7. When hiring a DJ, specify in the contract the exact name of the DJ who will be working the event and the exact starting time, the duration of the performance, and any extra charges that may be incurred. Discuss in advance the number of breaks that will be taken during the party and their lengths.

8. Not every DJ acts as an MC (master of ceremonies), so if you want a DJ to perform this task, make sure that this is agreed to in advance.

9. Make sure your DJ has directions to the location of the event.

10. Have the DJ check on the power availability of the location prior to the party so that there will be no on-site complications.

HIRING A BAND

Have you ever been to a party that had a bad, boring band playing? Can you think of anything worse to ruin a party? (Okay, bad, boring, bald waiters might beat out the battle of the bad band party killers, but . . .) There really isn't anything more torturous for guests than an awful band. It's much easier to hire a wretched band than any other type of entertainment. Hiring the right professional band for your event is one of the hardest tasks to accomplish in your planning process. *Finding* the right band is easier than *hiring* the right band. The best bands are booked so far in advance that often my clients have to make concessions to accommodate the band's availability. It's not uncommon for a band to be fully booked up to two years in advance, especially for Saturday night dates. If you decide that you want a band to entertain, *selecting* that band should be one of your first steps in the planning process.

Before you can find a band, you must first identify the style of music you want for your event. Clearly, different tones are set by the music for birthday parties, anniversary parties, and weddings. Some bands prefer to play more formal events, while others are better suited for more casual and laid-back parties. If your party has a theme, make sure you hire a band that adds to that creative atmosphere. If you're throwing a beach bash, a band that doesn't play "surfer" music might not be your best choice. At a minimum the band needs to know a few reggae tunes. On the flip side, a rocking party band might be a lot of fun for a graduation party but probably not your best choice for Mom and Dad's fiftieth wedding anniversary. Common sense and firsthand experience are your best guides. As you seek out a band for your affair, start paying attention to the entertainment at functions you attend. Note songs you like, songs you don't care for, style, presentation, and any other element that made a band memorable. If you want the band to play certain music, make sure you discuss the play list in advance of your event. Some bands may need to learn your special requests, so giving ample notice will help you enjoy your event from the "first dance" to the "last dance." Some clients like a band to talk in between songs, while other clients prefer sets that are played straight through with no interruption.

I am often asked to explain the music or live entertainment that is appropriate for different types of parties. What determines the hiring of a single or strolling musician, a band, a trio, a quartet, or an orchestra is the size of the venue and the gathering you're hosting. Single musicians, such as a flautist, violinist, harpist, or piano player, are commonly used before and during a wedding ceremony, at an anniversary party or a romantic dinner for two, or during a small cocktail reception. Smaller groups, such as a trio or quartet, are ideal for more intimate types of gatherings. Some of my clients opt to hire the smaller groups for cocktail receptions or dinner parties and then a larger band for the main reception, especially if dancing is part of the plan.

> **The Internet is a great place to check out entertainment acts. Be careful, though, because sometimes great Web sites can be deceiving. Always check references.**
>
> BEVERLY WARREN
> JERRY KRAVAT ENTERTAINMENT
> NEW YORK, NY

To find the musicians that are right for your occasion, check with local talent agencies and musicians' unions. If you are working with a party planner, he or she will have relationships with many of these organizations, musicians, and bands.

If you want to hire a band for your event, you may find the following ideas helpful:

1. Listen to demonstration tapes of the bands you are considering. Find out in advance how many members are in each band.

2. Get a complete list of equipment being provided by the band and any items you may need to furnish.

3. Negotiate the fee in advance. Discuss the length of the performance, the number of breaks, and wardrobe. Specify the exact

starting time, the duration of the performance, and any extra charges that may be incurred. Ask about any necessary deposit requirements.

4. Review the play list in advance of the event. Be sure to inform the band of any special requests prior to the party.

5. Find out what kind of music the band provides during breaks.

6. Ask if any special provisions need to be made to accommodate the band during the breaks.

7. Make sure the location for your event has the proper wiring and electrical requirements to handle all of the band equipment.

8. Make sure your band has directions to the location of the event.

9. Always check references.

ENTERTAINMENT ALTERNATIVES

Hosts are getting extremely creative when it comes to entertainment other than musicians. Celebrity look-alikes, belly dancers, glass blowers, acrobats, live animals, sports figures, motivational speakers, go-go dancers, classically trained performers, salsa dancers, clowns, magicians, psychics, puppets, karaoke, face painters, photo and video booths, and even Santa Claus are finding their way into neighbors' backyards these days. As themes for parties get more and more creative, hosts are relying less on music and musicians as the soul of the party and more on a combination of entertainers. Some innovative parties, such as a murder mystery event, do not need music; instead, actors are hired to help create a more realistic and believable atmosphere.

Choosing the perfect mix of entertainment for a party can be a little challenging, but, hey, that's why I'm here, right? Many of

In addition to providing great music and a big open space for dancing, bringing in professional dancers can take the excitement of a party to another level.

my clients want the mix of entertainment to give their parties that extra umph! You don't have to choose one type of entertainment for the entire evening. Be daring and bold. Think outside the box.

I attended a friend's birthday party on a yacht, and she insisted on keeping all her plans a secret, especially from me. As the boat sailed around Manhattan on a warm summer night, everyone was having a great time. My friend had chosen several of her favorite CDs, and the music was perfect for this summer sail. The yacht dropped anchor right in front of the Statue of Liberty, and our hostess started to make a toast. She thanked everyone for coming there and drew attention to the fabulous surroundings. She started to talk about people . . . people—who need people—and suddenly Barbra Streisand appeared out of nowhere and started serenading the crowd. This "Barbra" was actually a famed Streisand impersonator. Our hostess didn't tell a soul that the impersonator had boarded the ship before we left the dock, and she had kept him hidden in a stateroom belowdecks. This was a fantastic surprise memory for everyone who attended and is a perfect example of mixing your entertainment.

Budget is always a concern when planning a party, but your entertainment really is the heart of the entire event. In my opinion, it is not the place to skimp. Once you decide to throw a bash, have the chutzpah to really go for it! People want to have a good time, so allow your guests to cut loose and, above all, allow yourself the same opportunity

TOP *For a summer pool party, floating beach balls brighten up the water and give your guests something to play with.*

BOTTOM *A buffet of games and toys adds fun for adults as much as for kids.*

6 | Small Gatherings and Intimate Affairs

To get into the best society nowadays, one has either to
feed people, amuse people, or shock people.
—OSCAR WILDE

*Choose bright and cheery colors
for a garden breakfast. For the
centerpiece, a small cluster of all-
yellow flowers can be placed in
a milk bottle or pitcher you have
in your kitchen.*

Some of my favorite parties over the years have been the ones that
have been intimate gatherings. Romantic dinners for two, small cocktail parties, and Sunday brunch are just some of
the occasions that call for simple and informal
entertaining. Smaller gatherings should be
relaxed and fun to plan, and enjoyable for everyone to attend, including you! Knowing how to
achieve maximum results with minimum effort
is the secret to informal entertaining. These
events should be easy for you to plan on your
own. Memorable, magical, and marvelous are
the three Ms of simple and informal entertaining, and they are incorporated in the three parties featured in this chapter in distinctively
different ways. Each is easy to duplicate and
requires only your imagination, but sometimes
simple is better.

THE EVENT: A Romantic Fireplace Picnic for Two

THE SETTING A New York City town house.

THE CONCEPT As an extremely busy executive, my client wanted to plan a romantic tryst for himself and his wife, who had recently given birth to their first child. He hadn't spent a night alone romancing his wife since their baby was born, but now he had been able to arrange for some privacy so they could share a night of extravagance. We talked about his vision and came up with a picnic in front of the fireplace. It gave the sensation of being whisked away to a wonderful hideaway, while it offered the convenience of staying in comfortable surroundings. *Simple* and *elegant* were the two words my client kept mentioning when talking about this evening. Rose petals in pink, red, and white were scattered throughout the room. Large down pillows were placed in front of the fireplace to allow my client and his wife the greatest comfort while enjoying the roaring fire.

Chilled champagne, a roaring fire, and exotic foods guarantee an evening of romance.

THE LIGHTING Fifty candles of various sizes and shapes were lit throughout their home, offering a flickering golden hue. The fireplace added a magical natural light. Not too many scented candles were in the mix because the fragrance would have become overwhelming.

TUTERA TIP: A gorgeous variation on the votive candle can be created by carving out the center of a large rose bud, trimming the bottom flat, and nestling a small votive candle inside. A luscious glow emanates from within the flower.

THE FOOD Keeping with the spirit of romance, I planned an evening filled with erotic foods and sensual libations. Fresh strawberries with a chocolate fondue in silver serving dishes accompanied by a bottle of bubbly really got things going. The ice cubes that filled the crystal champagne bucket contained frozen fresh strawberries. The effect was marvelous. Exotic cheeses, caviar, and pâté were wonderfully presented on a masculine leather service platter. Green grapes surrounded the presentation, bringing the days of Caesar to Manhattan as my client's wife fed him grape after grape.

Planning a romantic evening like this is easy to do. It looks beautiful and will guarantee a night of passion! (For all you guys out there, think how pleased your wife or girlfriend will be to be surprised by such a feast!)

THE EVENT: Breakfast with the Ladies

THE SETTING The suburban home of a Chicago housewife.

NUMBER OF GUESTS Five.

THE CONCEPT Once a month these wonderful women make it a point to get together. They've been friends for many years and don't get the chance to keep up with the everyday details of one another's lives, so these mornings are cherished among the group. They keep every detail simple, which allows the hostess to enjoy maximum quality time with minimal effort.

THE MENU Assorted pastries, including chocolate croissants, fresh bagels, cinnamon buns, and fat-free muffins. Coffee, herbal tea, and juices served with fresh honey rounded out the simple menu.

THE FLOWERS One simple vase was filled with blue hydrangeas and yellow tulips. Tiny yellow zinnia heads embellished each place setting.

This breakfast party was organized to be as simple as possible for the hostess. The day before the event, I decorated my client's bright, sunny kitchen with items from her collections. All she had to do the next morning was put the pastries on the table and brew fresh coffee.

THE PLACE SETTING Various whimsical hand-painted Italian pottery dishes from the hostess's personal collection were used. Each plate was decorated with roosters and pigs, and the paper cocktail napkins were adorned with roosters, symbolic of the magical morning meeting.

A simple breakfast like this is an easy solution for entertaining a small group or a group of twenty or more. You can easily buy the pastries a day in advance and serve the meal buffet style. People get pleasure from entertaining, even if it's a simple breakfast that only requires making fresh coffee. Take pride in your presentation and put your efforts into a beautiful place setting or floral arrangement. Enjoying the company of favorite friends is always time well spent and an effort worth making.

COCKTAIL PARTIES

The cocktail party always reminds me of the decadent era of the 1920s because it was during Prohibition that cocktail parties became popular. Of course the addition of the Eighteenth Amendment to the Constitution didn't stop people from drinking; it merely changed who drank and how they acquired their alcohol. It also impacted where people consumed their cocktails and what they drank.

Speakeasies became underground bastions of business. Owners drew in crowds by creating an atmosphere of gaiety and offering an ample supply of the banned booze. Women were welcome in these establishments for the first time in the history of American alcohol consumption. Amazingly, prior to Prohibition, people considered drinking as something they did in their homes. But once liquor was considered contraband, it became necessary to think of new ways to distill, serve, and consume the stuff. When friends and family gathered for meals, it became commonplace to serve a cocktail before eating. Appetizers, such as tins of oysters, olives, and sardines, were served with the drinks, and by the end of the 1920s, women and men were whooping it up in a way that we now consider socially acceptable and downright fashionable.

Cocktail parties really hit their stride in the 1950s, when celebrities such as Frank Sinatra and Dean Martin glamorized the idea of sipping champagne or a martini while listening to Cole Porter on the phonograph. And who could ever forget the cocktail party scene from *Breakfast at Tiffany's* and Audrey Hepburn's wonderful portrayal of Holly Golightly, making it chic to enjoy a cocktail or two or ten.

Cocktail parties are more popular than ever now, and martinis have become the most popular drink; they come in more flavors than ice cream. Olives are now stuffed with garlic, anchovies, blue cheese, and pimentos. The word "cocktail" is so much a part of our vernacular that designers create special clothes suitable for cocktailing—cocktail attire, the perfect little black cocktail dress, the cocktail suit. Like a cocktail party, the look is appropriately short, sexy, and elegant.

THE CONCEPT When entertaining at home with a cocktail party, the design of the party should reflect the environment of your home. Numerous candles placed around the house and stunning floral

Put out only a small number of cocktail garnishes at a time to ensure that they stay fresh.

arrangements need to complement the interior design of the home. Make sure you move throughout the room and greet all your guests. A successful host is one who is a guest at his or her own party. A colleague of mine in the catering business once said that a real host never answers the door to his own cocktail party without having a drink in his hand. Your guests get the idea from that instant that this is supposed to be a festive few hours.

A black-tie cocktail party needs to be planned just as if you were planning a sit-down dinner. Invitations should be sent that include all the information required when hosting an evening dinner party. It is also very important to hire a caterer who is capable of servicing your needs. Remember, the service must be impeccable. Your guests should always have food and drink in hand, but only one hand. During this type of party, provide butlered food that should be served continuously. Beautifully garnished trays of food make a lasting impression regardless of what is being served. Guests should feel comfortable about eating and still feel elegant and chic while doing so.

Champagne is special enough, but floating raspberries in a sparkling glass adds color and fragrance and brightens the flavor of the champagne.

THE PERFECT MIX

THE GUESTS A successful cocktail party is about mingling and relaxing. Invite friends who mingle well together and keep the size appropriate for the venue. Too many people in a small room is never any fun. Likewise, too few people in a larger location makes the party seem impersonal and cold. When planning a cocktail party, the guest list is important, and you need to think carefully about who your guests will be. Inviting a mixture of people allows your guests to meet new people. New faces bring new topics of conversation. A good host continuously moves through the room. It is so important for everyone to feel special and comfortable.

THE INVITATION Whether you send a formal invitation or give a verbal invitation, always inform your guests in advance that you are hosting a cocktail party. Choosing the proper time to host a cocktail party is very important, and you should set both a starting and an ending time. This will help your guests plan their night. Some of them may be going on to another celebration.

THE ENTERTAINMENT The music should be cool and jazzy, and mostly of the instrumental variety for ambience. A collection of selected mixed music played on your cassette deck or compact disc player is important. A cocktail party is not the place for you to use a DJ. A single piano player is always a great mood setter for a cocktail party of any size. If you have the room, you can rent a piano. I had a client who did this once for a holiday cocktail party and loved the way the piano looked in her home so much that she ended up buying it! It turned out that the piano had a built-in disc player which automatically played music like an old-fashioned player piano. Think of all the money she saves by not having to blindfold the piano man!

THE FOOD Food is not the main focus of this type of party, though small finger food is highly recommended since it is an hour when people are getting hungry. I prefer hors d'oeuvres to be sparse when passed on a tray. It looks prettier and more appetizing than too much food, which can overwhelm guests. With less food on the trays, more staff than usual is required for there to be a constant flow. It's also important to make food available when serving alcohol. Passed food is the best option, and one stationary food station is also recommended. We have all been to a cocktail party where we tried to balance our drink and a plate of food with our two hands, while trying to eat standing up. That activity has provided hours of humorous entertainment for the other guests watching, but it's not fun! Which hand are you supposed to eat with if you're holding a plate *and* a cocktail anyway?

As a host I make sure that all preparations for food and drink have been made well in advance. You should never be seen running around getting drinks or running into the kitchen to get more hors d'oeuvres out of the oven. Try to keep your food selections simple and easy to serve; they should be able to sit in serving dishes once you've set them out. Anything that requires heating up should be served in chaffing pans that can remain heated throughout the party.

TUTERA TIP: I discourage smoking at any event, but it's a bit unrealistic to think that all guests will abide by such a request. Therefore, be sure to provide plenty of ashtrays throughout the space, and if at all possible, ask guests to smoke outside.

113

THE BEVERAGES Typically, cocktail parties are stocked with the most common liquor for pouring drinks. Vodka, gin, scotch, wine, champagne, and usually beer are the staples. Nonalcoholic drinks should always be offered as well, including soda, seltzer, juices, and bottled water. There is nothing wrong with serving specialty drinks as long as you prepare in advance. Make pitchers of margaritas instead of blending one at time. Have a blender or two on hand if you want to serve frozen drinks such as daiquiris or piña coladas. If planning a smaller gathering, make your bar area a self-service one. Glasses, alcohol, mixers, ice, lemons, limes, stirrers, and coasters are all out for guests to help themselves. You will find that guests feel more relaxed at smaller get-togethers when they can serve themselves.

THE PARTY HELP A server should offer the hors d'oeuvres with cocktail napkins, and a second staff member should immediately follow to provide cleanup for the guests. A bartender should be savvy at mixology. If you can't afford to hire party help such as cocktail servers and food servers or a bartender, set up a bar at one end of the room and a food station at the other end. This will keep the flow in constant motion.

Offer only one or two selections of hors d'oeuvres on a passing tray. By keeping the presentation simple, guests can quickly decide what they want.

BUTLERED HORS D'OEUVRES SUGGESTIONS

Louisiana Blackened Chicken with Bourbon Honey Mustard Sauce

Roasted Lobster on Corn Biscotti

Sesame Chicken in Spicy Peanut Sauce

Curried Lobster and Apple Tartlet

Blackened Fillet of Beef on Sourdough Rounds

Maryland Crab Cakes with Chesapeake Remoulade

Carolina Pork on Corn Cakes

Seared Sea Scallops with Fresh Lime Sambal

Ripe Melon Wrapped with Imported Prosciutto

Sautéed Shrimp Scampi

Indonesian Pork Satays with Bang-Bang Peanut Sauce

Seafood Quesadillas with Ricotta, Basil, and Lobster Oil

Lamb and Yucca Fritters with Coriander Yogurt Sauce

Smoked Irish Salmon on Buttered Black Bread

Miniature Veal Burgers with Red Onion Jam and Melted Fontina
on Toasted Brioche Rounds

Apple-Smoked Trout in Phyllo Cups with Sauce Raifort

Roasted Long Island Potatoes with Crème Fraîche and Caviar

Pepper-Crusted Loin of Tuna with Cilantro Aioli on Gyoza Crisps

Sesame-Crusted Chicken Maki with Red Chili Dipping Sauce

Potato Pancakes with Crème Fraîche and Applesauce

Ginger Chicken Dumplings in Plum Sauce

Cinnamon and Maple Roasted Sweet Potato Cups

Chicken and Apple Sausage Strudels with Preserved Fruit Chutney
and Fresh Thyme

Pear and Cranberry Compote with Melted Gruyère Cheese

Woodland Mushroom Strudels

Endive Leaves with Curried Chicken

Parmesan and Walnut Twists

Truffled Risotto Cakes

Endive with Curried Vegetables

Homemade Spirals of Mozzarella, Oven-Roasted Tomato, and Basil
on Toasted Focaccia Croustades

Wild Mushroom Ravioli with Smoked Tomato Chutney

*Keep your hors d'oeuvres man-
ageable in size—easy handling
is crucial at any cocktail party.*

7 | Birthday Parties

A day is a year is a lifetime is an age.
—ANONYMOUS

Birthdays are part of the grand cycle of life. Like it or not, we all have one. When considering the symbolic meaning of celebrating a person's date of birth, three important areas are often studied and compared to make up the circular framework of life: human life, astrology, and nature. For humans the circle represents a lifetime—from birth to death. In astrology the zodiac is always depicted as a circle. In nature the four seasons make up the cycle of a calendar year. I selected three parties to illustrate the beautiful celebration of all three.

Celebrate the cycles of life: Plan a birthday party for yourself or someone you love.

Birthdays. Any way you look at them, some people love this special day, while others would prefer it to come and go quietly. I, of course, seek the client who loves to celebrate. The most important thing to remember when planning a birthday for you or someone else is to make sure it reflects the personality of the honoree. Whoever it is for, keep the mood festive and make the event memorable.

117

THE EVENT: A Fiftieth Birthday Party

THE SETTING Weekend country home in Pound Ridge, New York.

THE GUESTS Eighty close friends and family members.

THE CONCEPT This party takes first place for one of the most elaborate and intimate birthday celebrations. My client, the wife of a prominent New York businessman, spared no expense to ensure that this would be a party to remember. Everything from the linens to the decorations was custom made for the party. Nothing was store-bought or mass-produced. The home where the party was to be held was surrounded with magnificent wild-flower gardens. I wanted to take full advantage of their grandeur and beauty in my design for the event, but the party also had to reflect my client's husband, which meant keeping the elements masculine. I erected a clear tent over the entire garden area, guaranteeing that rain or shine the guests would be able to enjoy the gardens. It rained and stormed just prior to the party, and there was a concern that it would have to be moved inside. As guests started to arrive, there was a tremendous downpour. Shortly thereafter, just as the string quartet hired for the evening began to play, the skies cleared up and the rain stopped. It was like a scene from a Hollywood movie, and one even I could not have planned any more dramatically. There was never a moment of concern for anyone's safety because I always insist on using the best-quality tenting and lighting companies that have the expertise to handle unexpected weather conditions.

Add some fun to small gatherings (especially a birthday party) by mixing up your guest list. Rather than having table assignments, do the following: Take two containers (one for men, the other for women) and have each person draw a card that contains a picture. They will then sit at the table displaying that same picture. Your job as host is to predetermine the mixture of males and females at each table, which can be quite eclectic. Birthdays are great for this since everyone in attendance is honoring the same person, and therefore they all have something in common.

118

For a spring or summer table, you can make a wonderful runner and centerpiece with sections of slate from your local garden center edged with wheat grass.

THE LIGHTING As evening approached, the specially installed lighting around the property was illuminated, creating a stunning ethereal effect. The hues ranged from soft lavender to more vibrant pinks and yellows, perfectly emulating the botanical arrangements used throughout the party space. The interior of the tent, which contained all the wild gardens, was also specially lit for the evening with tiny tea lights, bringing the starlight feel inside the room as if the night sky were within reach of an outstretched hand.

THE TABLE SETTING The objective was for each table's ambience to suggest a dinner for ten rather than dinner for eighty. Each of the eight guest tables was a rectangular-shaped antique, and I felt it served no purpose to use them and then cover them with tablecloths. I therefore customized linen place mats for each place setting. The feel was intimate and special. Rented antique tapestry chairs were placed around each table, adding a sense of warmth and a homey feel to the outdoor setting and giving a distinctive look. A raised runner of slate, framed by wheat grass and mosses, ran down the center of each table. Antique mahogany candlesticks and custom-made mica lampshades were purchased for each table. In the center of the runner I placed dark antique wooden bowls and filled them with light green apples, a unique alternative to standard floral centerpieces. The final accents for the tables were tall sections of beach grass, which added height to the centerpieces, and scattered light green orchid heads, which softened the lines of the slate. We used two different styles of china, a copper charger plate and a whitewashed terra-cotta first-course plate. For the rest of the meal, plain white china was used. Custom-made cream-colored napkins tied with burlap ribbon adorned each place setting.

THE ENTERTAINMENT To embrace the romantic setting, I chose a four-piece string quartet to play music for the entire evening. The quartet performed from a raised platform overlooking the room.

THE FOOD Tuscan cuisine was featured. This was the menu:

HORS D'OEUVRES

Roasted lobster and corn bisque

Seared sea scallops with fresh sambal

Roasted potatoes with crème fraîche and caviar

Potato pancakes with applesauce

Five-spice duck and cabbage rolls

Large chilled shrimp served with traditional cocktail sauce

Blackened chicken with bourbon honey mustard

Phyllo cups of apple-smoked trout

BUFFET DINNER MENU

FIRST COURSE

Chilled Tuscan vegetable soup

ENTREES

Individual grilled Capri steak

New potatoes with fennel and pine nuts

Asparagus and corn salad with truffle oil

Tuscan fried chicken

Seared filet of wild striped bass served with aromatic vegetables in herbed broth

Vine-ripened heirloom tomatoes and Gorgonzola with a balsamic vinaigrette

Yellow squash, zucchini, roasted red and yellow peppers

Layers of herbed polenta with roasted vegetables and fresh mozzarella, topped with broiled sundried tomatoes and aged Parmigiano-Reggiano cheese

DESSERTS

A selection of saint ambrosia (mixture of fruit, marshmallows, and coconut)

Sorbet, gelato, and ice cream

Miniature chocolate cups, pastry cups, cones, and small bowls, accompanied by raspberry, hot chocolate, and butterscotch sauces

Chef's selection of biscotti, cookies, and truffles

Dessert at a birthday party needs to be spectacular. In this case, the brilliant cake creator Sylvia Weinstock baked a gorgeous confection topped with sugar flowers.

Tuscan food is perfect for a warm summer soiree. It is light and very flavorful. I chose to have the first course served at the table and the rest of the meal buffet style. I do this a lot to encourage mingling among the guests, especially in more intimate settings. The buffet tables were carefully placed within the gardens, and each was covered with sod and moss to keep the feeling of actually being in the gardens. All the serving dishes were placed on slate and moss to match the centerpieces of the dining tables. I also purchased white serving platters and had them hand-painted with colorful floral designs to add a dash of vibrancy.

Since this was a birthday party, dessert had to be breathtaking. Eight individual birthday cakes were brought out, one to each table, again giving the impression of a more intimate dinner. Ice cream was served French style, with guests choosing chocolate or vanilla. Miniature pastries placed on antique mahogany trays were set on each table.

This was truly an evening of elegance in a spectacular summer garden setting. The guests were certainly aware of the time and effort that went into every aspect of the planning, and everyone, especially the birthday boy, had a marvelous time.

THE EVENT: A Contemporary Bat Mitzvah

THE SETTING The spacious backyard of the family estate in Greenwich, Connecticut.

THE GUESTS Two hundred (one hundred children and one hundred adults).

THE CONCEPT "Looking into the Future," since in the Jewish religion, when a child turns thirteen, it is a symbolic passing from childhood into adulthood. I created the theme of this party around the idea that the young honoree was leaving her childhood behind and heading toward her future. The home in which this party took place is a dramatic estate resembling a European castle, so my real challenge was coming up with a concept that would not detract from the grandeur of the home. Knowing that the party would be primarily based in the backyard, I decided that designing in the opposite direction of the architecture would have the greatest impact when guests arrived. I chose a futuristic space-inspired design, successfully mixing old with new. I tented the backyard with an enormous 100-by-60-foot enclosed tent. This black-tie evening affair transported guests into the future as they entered. Twenty tables of ten were set in colorful and whimsical patterns. White spandex tubes reached from the floor to the ceiling throughout the space and were lit from within, allowing for constantly changing colors as the party progressed. Lime green, fuchsia, purple, yellow, and blue directed the color scheme for everything. White spheres, 6 feet in diameter, hung from the ceiling and were splashed with coordinating theatrical lighting.

THE TABLE SETTINGS All the tables were lit in neon, appearing to be illuminated from underneath, and then covered with sheer pewter tablecloths. The effect gave the tables a crystal-ball–like appearance.

The simple addition of inexpensive colorful daisies at each place setting created a whimsical air.

The overall look resembled something you might find in an MTV music video, appropriate for a party for a thirteen-year-old. Keeping with that idea, the centerpieces were simple glass blocks stacked in a mound and surrounded by daisies hand-dyed in the same lively colors as the lighting. Each table was lit with an individual pin spotlight, giving the illusion that the glass blocks were lit from within. This was a very economical centerpiece and is very easy to duplicate. Glass blocks are available at any home improvement store and are easy to work with. The parents of the honoree chose to put their money into the theatrics of the space and the entertainment instead of the table settings, a decision with which I concurred. Place settings were not what the young girl's friends would remember. Each place setting was eclectic and fun, mixing and matching various colored glassware. The pewter-colored napkins were accented with multicolored daisies to match the centerpieces.

THE MENU Hot dogs, hamburgers, chicken nuggets, pizza, French fries, and onion rings.

Kids' parties are for the kids, and therefore the menu needs to be aimed at the young revelers. I have found that chicken nuggets, pizza, hamburgers, and pasta are the easiest choices and for the most part satisfy the kids' appetites. It's no coincidence that many of the adults end up sneaking a bite or two of the kids' fare, though few will admit it. When planning a bar or bat mitzvah where even numbers of adults and children are attending, I plan a menu that works for both groups. Food is rarely a priority for the younger set. For dessert, a traditional celebration cake was served, and a fabulous ice cream sundae bar was positioned at the rear of the tent. Ice cream bars are a hit at any party but are especially suited for a celebration for kids of all ages.

THE ENTERTAINMENT A live DJ, MTV-style dancers, psychic readers, and fortune-tellers were hired, in keeping with the "Looking into the Future" theme. The psychics and fortune-tellers gave readings to guests about the future. People love astrology and psychic phenomena, and these gifted people always provide a wonderful type of entertainment at any event. The choice of using a DJ provided the sounds and music that the kids are most familiar with. Dancing also

helps to get the older crowd mingling with the kids. The DJ got everyone up and dancing and kept the spirits high throughout the evening.
In a party of this nature, there is usually a candle-lighting ceremony,
a tradition in Jewish ceremonies. The DJ acted as master of ceremonies for this custom.

When planning this party I was able to replicate somewhat the
theme I used for the Grammy Awards post-party. My clients had seen
photographs of the Grammy party and fell in love with several of the
elements. That party had been planned for three thousand guests.
Downsizing it to custom-fit my clients' needs and budget was an interesting challenge, but one I think we met brilliantly. The bat mitzvah girl
had a great time with her friends, and the proud parents were able to
celebrate the joyous event in a style they chose and could enjoy.

*These white spandex tubes had
up-lights installed inside so that
they glowed from within. The
lights also changed colors.*

THE EVENT: A First Birthday Party

THE SETTING The local dog park.

THE GUESTS Eight fuzzy friends of various breeds.

THE HOST Pug.

METHOD OF PAYMENT *Master*Card (get it?).

THE INVITATION A small bag of dry dog food with a custom label inviting guests and their owners to attend the celebration.

THE CONCEPT The owner of the pug called me to ask if I'd consider doing this job, and I was amused at the prospect. I had always wanted to throw a party for a family pet because I am an avid animal lover. I suggested celebrating this canine coronation with a carnival theme fit for a king.

THE ENTERTAINMENT I hired a *master* of ceremonies who kept all the animals amused with ring toss games and Frisbee fetch competitions. The owners of the animals went right along with the carnival theme by playing various games at booths that had been set up. Clowns, jugglers, magicians, and a roving mandolin player entertained the guests, young and old. The entertainers were dressed in Renaissance-era clothing. All the puppy partyers wore cone-shaped party hats and were supplied with noise-making squeaky toys.

King for a day . . .

THE MENU A three-course feast served in personalized doggy dishes: hound dogs wrapped in organic phyllo, puppy pâté pop-ups, and beefy biscuits. Human guests were served "bark-b-q" ribs and chicken, corn on the cob, cole slaw, and warm rolls.

The joy in planning this party was that it was really celebrating something different—the love between an owner and his animal. There was no precedence for this party, and if I had to do it all over again, I wouldn't change a thing. Not everyone is suited to hosting such an extravagant affair for his or her pooch, but the idea can easily be used for another type of festivity. It was a simple party to coordinate, and everyone had a great time. There was something for everyone in attendance, human and nonhuman.

*W*hen hosting a birthday party, try to incorporate the flower and/or birthstone of the honoree into the table setting or overall design of the party. Imagine a March birthday party designed with the tablecloths in all aqua and the flowers in the center all violets. It is a terrific way to personalize the party while adding character to the concept as well. A handwritten note or description tied to color-coordinated paper and ribbon can be attached to the pretty nosegay of flowers for guests to read.

BIRTHDAY STONES AND FLOWERS

MONTH	STONE	FLOWER
January	Garnet	Carnation
February	Amethyst	Primrose
March	Aquamarine	Violet
April	Diamond	Daisy or lily
May	Emerald	Lily of the valley
June	Pearl or moonstone	Rose
July	Ruby	Sweet pea
August	Peridot	Gladiolus
September	Sapphire	Aster
October	Opal	Dahlia
November	Topaz or citrine	Chrysanthemum
December	Turquoise or lapis lazuli	Poinsettia

8 | Weddings

This chapter can in no way be considered a total wedding planner; I could easily write an entire book on the subject. My goal in the following pages is to help you get creative in the planning process. Many of my clients are mothers of the bride and groom and the bride herself. This chapter is intended to inspire something in everyone involved in the wedding.

For most people the biggest party they will ever be involved in planning is their wedding day. With few exceptions, this is the one time in your life that you will want to go all out. Weddings come in all shapes and sizes. I have found that no matter what your limitations are, the magnificence is in the attention to detail. To me, weddings are sophisticated and elegant events. I always encourage my clients to create an atmosphere of intimacy. After all, getting married is a very personal moment in a couple's life. It's a day of bringing their closest family and friends together to witness as well as celebrate their union. The event should be a reflection of the couple's personality, making it a special and memorable experience for everyone.

When planning a wedding with my clients, I focus on four main areas: the elegance of the invitation; the fantasy of the decor, including table settings and breathtaking floral designs; the delicacy of the food; and the atmosphere and energy set by the entertainment. Ironically, the party often overshadows the ceremony itself, but the

Aside from the bride's dress, nothing gets as much attention on a wedding day as a gorgeous cake.

ABOVE *The menu cards on the tables were coordinated with the overall design of the wedding.*

OPPOSITE *White lace and white china make a beautiful old-fashioned wedding table.*

ceremony is really the most important part of the day. I strongly encourage my clients to seek some unique element that adds a personal touch to their ceremony. We often put an emphasis on flowers, music, or setting to add a little panache.

The most important rule when planning a wedding is that there are no rules or boundaries. Many of my clients come to me with the notion that they have to do certain things when making their wedding day plans. I try gently to encourage ideas that go beyond the limit my client has set in his and her mind. The client should take every opportunity to infuse his or her own personal ideas and reflections into each element of the day.

For most, the wedding day is the culmination of a childhood fantasy come true. Think about it like this: A wedding lasts just a few hours, a marriage is for a lifetime. The planning process takes months; how you spend that time should be as memorable and enjoyable as the party itself. Too many times the planning process becomes a source of aggravation among families as well as the bride and groom. I try to instill a sense of celebration from the first meeting with the couple and encourage them to maintain that same feeling through the big day.

Creating a comfort level from the beginning of the planning process is the key to keeping things light and fun—and sane. Believe me when I say that I've played referee many times over battles that in the end simply didn't matter. The average cost of a wedding today is approximately $19,000. When you're spending that kind of money, it's important to get everything you want without compromise.

There are some very important matters to consider before you start the ball rolling. First and foremost, set a budget. How much do you plan to spend to create this magical day? Once you've made that decision, everything else is worked into that formula. Decide on the style of wedding you want. Will it be a large affair or an intimate gathering? How formal do you want the ceremony and reception? Will it be a daytime or an evening event? What dates are you considering? The season in which the wedding takes place affects the type of wedding you plan. Whether you are planning a wedding or any other type of party, the basic plan of action is the same as discussed previously in this book. What distinguishes a wedding are the distinctive elements that personalize this special day.

BRIDAL BOUQUETS

Bridal bouquets are generally designed to match the style of the bride's dress. It used to be that if the bride wore white, the bouquet had to be white, but that is no longer the case. Personal style has introduced more and more interesting selections of color and theme into the wedding flowers, especially when it comes to the bride's bouquet. Simplicity is my signature when selecting bouquet arrangements.

Bouquets must work not only with the bride's dress but also with the bride's proportions. A petite bride shouldn't carry a bouquet resembling a large Olympic torch. Likewise, a statuesque bride shouldn't look like Lady Liberty. Every detail needs to be considered in this selection. I always ask the bride for a sketch or photograph of the dress she will be wearing so I can match the details of the bouquet to her dress. For example, if there is pearl beading on the dress, I will include pearl beading in the bouquet. If the dress has a lot of lace, I will use lace in the bouquet design.

The shape of a bouquet can range from full and round to tall and narrow. The round hand-tied bouquet is the most popular selection. Cascading bouquets are a lot more dramatic but cannot be pulled off by every bride. The teardrop shape is in between the two and is less formal. There is also the cradle style, which is my least favorite. I think a bride should look comfortable and elegant, and this style is clumsy and awkward looking unless you're Miss America.

Roses, the most common flowers used in bridal bouquets, come in the largest variety of colors. Working with roses is similar to picking a shade of paint these days. Growers are cross-pollinating new colors all the time. The spectrum runs from pure white to lavender, terra-cotta, and even black (though I'd never recommend black roses for a bride). Another unique option is the nonfloral bridal bouquet, made from a selection of various fruits and herbs.

Bridal bouquets can vary in size, shape, color, and design, but they should generally match the bride's dress and the overall look of the wedding. Think of the bouquet as an accessory, just as you would shoes, a handbag, or jewelry.

133

If possible, have your dress-maker give you extra fabric from the wedding gown (or material left over from alterations) to use as the stem wrapping for the bridal bouquet. It customizes the arrangement and gives it a matching look. If you have enough yardage, you can use it on the bridesmaids' bouquets as well.

Bridesmaids' bouquets should not exactly match the bride's arrangement but should complement it. The bride's bouquet should always be larger and have a quality that distinguishes it, such as a slightly different flower or color. The groom's boutonniere should be a piece extracted from the bride's bouquet, as should those of the groomsmen and ushers. Don't be afraid to let the men wear a colored flower. It can add a sense of style and frivolity to a traditional choice.

The following are favorite flowers for a bridal bouquet:

Calla lilies

Dahlias

Freesias

Herbs (lamb's ears, rosemary, sage, or tansy)

Hyacinths

Lilacs

Lilies of the valley

Narcissus

Orchids

Pansies

Peonies

Poppies

Queen Anne's lace

Ranunculus

Roses

Scabiosa

Stars of Bethlehem

Stephanotis

Stock

Sweet peas

Tulips

WEDDING CAKE

The wedding cake is traditionally one of the most dramatic elements in a wedding reception. The cake is often displayed for guests to admire, and the cutting of the cake is a highlight for every bride and groom. The significance of eating cake at a wedding dates as far back as the Roman Empire. Romans made simple barley cakes and crumbled them over the bride's head for fertility. In the Middle Ages small sweet buns were traditionally brought to the bride and groom by guests and stacked before the couple, who would try to kiss over the mound as a sign of prosperity and a hope for a large family. Fantasy cakes are a recent development in the history of weddings. The more elaborate cakes are virtually great works of art. The most famous wedding cake designer and baker is Sylvia Weinstock. I have had the pleasure of working with her often and asked her what trends she has noticed in the world of wedding cakes. This was her response:

ABOVE *This cake was decorated in shades of blue to match the ice blue of the bride's gown.*

OPPOSITE *Small cakes are a wonderful touch for each guest.*

Today people have a more sophisticated palate; they choose cakes that reflect their personalities, such as a hazelnut cake with a mocha filling. The traditional white cake with white frosting is out for weddings I'm doing. As far as the look, people are choosing bolder colors for wedding cakes. The seasons affect the choice. In the fall the colors are bold; in the summer the colors are more vivid; and in the spring the colors are more muted.

I always try to coordinate some element of the wedding design into the design of the cake—color scheme or floral motif, for example. Some cake designers can make sugar-dough flowers that look so real, you'd swear they are actually fragrant. I still use the common figurine of the bride and groom from time to time, but the variations and selections available to most brides and grooms today offer a far more creative option. Layers and multiple tiers that combine different shapes and sizes make the wedding cake a truly inventive centerpiece. Guests enjoy sharing the symbolic happiness almost as much as they appreciate the delicious flavors. Cakes should be irresistibly edible, inside and out.

People are looking for cakes that are distinctive. Rolled fondant is getting bigger here in the United States, like it is in Europe and the U.K. We like to use it because it stands out, allowing us to work in a more artistic medium and add more detail.

STEVE MARONIAN
SWEET LISA'S EXQUISITE
CAKES
NEW YORK, NY

137

THE EVENT: The Wedding of Elizabeth and John

THE SETTING Home of the bride's family.

THE GUESTS Two hundred friends and family.

THE CONCEPT This wedding was a very special night designed to keep the guests moving through three separate tented areas. The ceremony took place under one tent, cocktails were around the pool, and the reception moved into a second tented area that was the main tent for the evening. The tent was transformed into a space with an exotic Middle Eastern flair. The first tented area was then converted to a dessert and coffee lounge.

For a spectacular first course, crabmeat and avocado were stacked with crisp plantain chips and set in a vinaigrette of red and yellow tomatoes topped with crème fraîche and sevruga caviar.

THE CEREMONY As a wedding planner I face many challenges, but one of the trickiest to finesse is that of an interfaith ceremony. In this particular case, the bride wanted to represent her Jewish heritage and the groom his Persian heritage without one overshadowing the other. Instead of the traditional canopy, or chupah, typically used during a Jewish ceremony, I built a gazebo for the ceremony to take place under and created a fantasy garden setting under a tent. I utilized the symbolic items usually associated with a Persian ceremony, such as the ceremonial rug known as a *safray,* by displaying them directly in front of the gazebo. The ceremony itself was designed to draw the guests into a fantasy setting. The yard had a dramatic fountain, so I used it to draw attention to the ceremony. I placed fragrant gardenias all around the fountain, which scented the tent all evening long, and additional shrubs and trees added a true garden quality.

An abundance of lanterns were suspended overhead at various heights, panels of gold-beaded fabric were installed to add a soft touch, and huge bursts of flowers were also hung within the tent to add texture and warmth to the atmosphere.

THE COCKTAILS After the ceremony, guests were ushered to the pool area, the focus for the cocktail hour. Drinks and hors d'oeuvres were passed. Silver trays were minimally garnished with roses and gardenias, and the simplicity made for an elegant hour.

THE RECEPTION The reception took place in a third tented area, the main party location for the rest of the night. This tent was located across the pool, and was visible when guests entered. During the cocktail hour, the dinner tent remained closed on all sides. As the guests started to make their way to the tent for the reception, I removed the entire front side, revealing the interior. The dramatic effect set the tone for a magical evening. The band maintained the festive mood by playing Middle Eastern music as the guests made their way to the tables. The wait staff was placed around the entire perimeter of the tent as everyone entered, and the effect was sensational. It sent a clear message that service was going to be above and beyond expectations.

THE TABLE SETTING The bride, a professional photographer, wanted an artistic and photogenic look to the room. Each of the twenty tables of ten was completely different in design. The unusual mosaic vases used as centerpieces were filled with exotic, richly colored flowers accented with sliced fresh fruit. The ceiling was decorated with stained-glass lanterns which added a deep romantic glow.

ABOVE *Dried fruit in a gold mesh pouch was provided to guests as favors.*

OPPOSITE *To add a unique touch to the bride and groom's chairs, a swag of flowers matching the bridal bouquet was draped along the back.*

THE MENU

PASSED HORS D'OEUVRES

Marinated Lamb on Crispy Lentil Wafers

Tartlets of Roasted Fennel, Tomato, and Feta

Grape Leaves Stuffed with Couscous, Feta, and Pine Nuts

Endive with Hummus and Roasted Peppers

FIRST COURSE

Tomato and Mint Salad

Hummus and Baba Ghanoush with Pita Triangles

MAIN COURSE

Lamb Kebobs with Toasted Cumin and Coriander

Roasted Quince Chutney

Rice Pilaf with Pine Nuts, Currants, and Cinnamon

Ragout of Artichokes and Fava Beans

DESSERT

Frozen Honey Yogurt with Cardamom

Roasted Peaches and Apricots

THE EVENT: The Wedding of Karen and Steve

The flowers used in this tall centerpiece were bold and bright, adding a punch of excitement to both the guest tables and the overall party space.

THE SETTING A photographer's studio in New York City.

THE GUESTS One hundred friends and family.

THE CONCEPT The bride and groom lived in the suburbs, but all their family and friends lived in Manhattan, so they chose to celebrate their wedding in New York City. The wedding took place over the Fourth of July weekend, and the bride and groom wanted to incorporate that festive element into the design without limiting the color scheme to red, white, and blue. Rather than a traditional setting, they opted for an urban and more avant-garde setting on the Hudson River that reflected their artistic backgrounds. The groom is a writer, and the bride works as a graphics designer. The decision to add a bold color scheme to the wedding design was also less traditional, especially for a second wedding. In fact, other than the walls and floor of the space itself, the bride and groom asked me not to incorporate white in any of the design. This was even carried out in the bride's dress selection; it was pewter. That color was therefore used in every detail of the wedding and reception.

THE TABLE SETTING The linens and table settings were very contemporary in design, and color was the number-one tool used to create a truly joyous atmosphere. Three different colors of glassware were selected: lime green, sky blue, and canary yellow. The charger plate was frosted white, the salad plate was frosted yellow, and the main course plate had a green swirl pattern. The pewter linens, carefully placed in two layers, had a satin underlay, and an organza overlay. Each napkin held a nosegay of coordinating flowers. The matching pewter chairs had gray cushions and were entirely covered with sheer organza and had a floral nosegay matching the napkins attached to the back. The overall effect was festive and fun, and visually it was unlike any ordinary wedding.

THE FLOWERS A combination of high and low arrangements was selected to give an ebb-and-flow effect to the design. Silver containers held the centerpieces, which were bursting with vibrant seasonal flowers, including bright blue hydrangeas; canary yellow calla lilies; lavender tulips; bright purple anemones; hot pink, fire red, and orange roses; and yellow onecium orchids accented by rust-colored kangaroo paw. The effect was that of exploding fireworks. If the flowers glowed, it would have looked like the Fourth of July.

THE ENTERTAINMENT A jazz quartet entertained the guests throughout the evening. It was a perfect combination for the style and location of the wedding. The couple did not want a dance-oriented affair, so they selected musical accompaniment that lent itself to the backdrop of the city as well as the ambience of the loft. The bride and groom are also enormous jazz enthusiasts, so the entertainment infused their personality into the party.

TUTERA TIP: Throwing rice at wedding ceremonies is no longer common practice. But guests should have fun when the happy couple walks by after the ceremony, such as blowing bubbles in the breeze or throwing beautiful flower blossoms. A more colorful and seasonal approach can be added to this ceremonial custom: In the spring, have baskets of loose flower heads that are in season. Loose petals of roses or hydrangeas are perfect. For the summer, sunflower petals or wax flower daisy heads are wonderful. During autumn, have pressed autumn-colored leaves available to toss into the air. The winter is a good time for white paper snowflakes. A paper cutter that can be used to obtain snowflake shapes is easily available at any arts and crafts store. Prepackage these wintry snowflakes in clear or frosted paper pouches tied with white ribbons.

Accessorizing each napkin with the same types of flowers used in the table arrangement gives a burst of color to the entire table.

143

MORE WEDDING TRADITIONS: CHEERS AND OTHER TOASTS

Weddings are always a time for friends and family to raise their glasses to the bride and groom and to share with others their thoughts, feelings, memories, and advice. But who should offer a toast, and when is the right time? Clients frequently ask me what's proper and expected when it comes to toasting. Since every wedding is a personal event, the rules of etiquette are not absolute, but the following guide will ensure that your toasts are appropriate and timely.

A good time to toast is at the rehearsal dinner. Generally speaking, the rehearsal dinner is a smaller, more informal gathering. Because it is more intimate than the reception, it is often a great time to share your thoughts and wishes with the happy couple. If the father of the groom wishes to propose a toast to the couple, the rehearsal dinner is the appropriate time to do so. In addition, the bride and groom may toast each other, their parents, and the bridal party. Members of the bridal party or close relatives and friends may also use this time to share their blessings and well wishes. Some couples have a toast or two, while others have many more. Remember, this is your event, so the choice is yours—but try to keep the toasts short and sweet.

Toasts at the wedding reception are an important tradition. It is a time for those closest to the bride and groom to give their blessings on the marriage. Traditionally, it is the duty of the best man to capture the attention of the guests and propose a toast to the bride and groom. His toast may be the only one offered, or he may be followed by the groom, who generally thanks his best man, parents, and guests, and then proposes a toast to his bride. In some cases the bride follows the groom to thank him and the guests and then proposes a toast to her parents and new in-laws. Frequently the

ABOVE *Frame your menu cards with coordinating colors to create a custom-made effect.*

OPPOSITE *Placing rose petals in various colors in a bowl can be a simple and elegant touch at each place setting.*

Weddings are overwhelmingly associated with white, but this design makes a romantic and exotic statement by using hot pink and orange with touches of gold.

father of the bride proposes a toast on behalf of his wife and himself, sharing his thoughts on the momentous occasion and thanking the guests for attending the wedding.

Regardless of who is proposing the toast, there are certain guidelines to follow:

If you are toasting, before you begin, make sure that all glasses have been filled, including your own. The bride should be served first, then the groom, maid of honor, parents, and the best man. You should be standing, with the glass in your right hand. Upon finishing the toast, raise your glass, clink glasses with others, and then sip the beverage.

If you are being toasted, remain seated as the guests rise in your honor. You should not raise your glass or sip from it when you are being toasted. When the toast is finished, you should graciously smile to acknowledge the toast and thank the toaster.

SHALL WE DANCE?

One of the most common questions I am asked when planning a wedding is about the couple's first dance. It's a moment that brides and grooms keep forever etched in their minds. It is one of their first experiences as husband and wife. But for many it is a source of angst. To help alleviate the anxiety of having all eyes on them, I often suggest that my clients enroll in a ballroom dance class to sharpen their dance skills. It's also a great stress buster in the planning process. It's an activity that connects the couple, and dancing is, like riding a bicycle, something they'll never forget once they've learned it.

Selecting the proper music is also key to a successful first dance. Some couples like to keep the song romantic, while others like to liven up the party and set a really fun tone for the rest of the reception. It's totally up to you. Whatever feels good is the best choice.

TUTERA TIP: It's a wonderful idea for the bride and groom to write their own wedding vows. The ceremony is the perfect time to share their heartfelt thoughts of each other. Each element of the wedding offers an opportunity to express a personal sentiment and something meaningful about their relationship. Telling a short story of how they met or when they knew they were in love can make the most special of days even more so. Brides and grooms tend to worry more about the reception than the ceremony. Remember, the ceremony is the time that truly belongs to the couple. This is a celebration of their love and commitment to one another.

*T*UTERA'S TOP TEN WEDDING CEREMONY MUSIC SELECTIONS

1. *Wedding March* by Felix Mendelssohn or Richard Wagner

2. *Canon in D Minor* by Johann Pachelbel

3. "Spring" from *The Four Seasons* by Antonio Vivaldi

4. "Musetta's Waltz" from *La Bohème* by Giacomo Puccini

5. "All I Ask of You" by Andrew Lloyd Webber

6. *Trumpet Voluntary* by Henry Purcell

7. *Jesu, Joy of Man's Desiring* by Johann Sebastian Bach

8. *Water Music* by George Frederic Handel

9. *Toccata* and *Fugue in D Minor* by Johann Sebastian Bach

10. *Ave Maria* (any version)

TUTERA TIP: If you are using ceremony programs, have them displayed in a beautiful open paper pouch that matches the design of the wedding. Also, using a simple satin ribbon, tie one to the inside of each guest's chair at the ceremony. This is wonderful for an outdoor ceremony because the programs stay secure and will not blow away in the wind.

CHOOSING A PHOTOGRAPHER

Your photographer captures your memories and creates the album that becomes a family heirloom. Choosing the right photographer for your wedding makes a difference in the years to come!

The first step in finding a photographer for your wedding is to ask friends and family members for recommendations. Then make an appointment to meet with the photographer and see his or her portfolio. You don't need to know a lot about photography to judge the quality of the work. Look at some of the photos as a way of getting a sense of the photographer's style. It's simple: If you like what was done for other couples, then you'll probably like what will be done for you.

While looking over the portfolio, take a moment to size up the photographer's personality as well. This person is going to be following you around all day, so you had better make sure you don't mind the company! If for some reason you don't like the person's approach or what you see in the portfolio, then follow your instincts and look around for another photographer.

The three main differences among wedding photographers are experience, price, and style. Although each has a unique style, most fall into three main categories: fashion photographers, formal portrait photographers, and photojournalists.

Fashion photographers take pictures of couples in relaxed but staged settings. These photos tend to highlight the emotions of the wedding day and often focus on how a couple looks and interacts together. This type of photographer often wants to schedule a "shoot" the day of the wedding at a particularly scenic location.

Formal portrait photographers take pictures with a classic, timeless quality. Portrait photographs do an excellent job of recording an important event in your life in images that can serve as valuable heirlooms in the years to come.

Photojournalists take a less structured approach to the wedding day. Their photos have a high degree of artistic quality and tend to capture quieter moments to tell a story. Typically, a wedding photojournalist does not take such standard shots as the extended family together with the bride and groom at the altar. Characteristic photos in a wedding photojournalist's portfolio might include the bride talking to her father as they wait to walk down the aisle or the bride and groom sharing a private conversation after the reception.

Many photographers offer a combination of these three styles or let you choose among them. If you can't get a sense of a photographer's style from looking at his or her portfolio, it is important to ask.

It has become increasingly popular to complement professional photographs with snapshots taken by family and friends. If you like, you can include a disposable camera on each table at the reception and encourage your friends to take photos. These candid and fun photos are a perfect accompaniment to the beautiful and artistic photos taken by your professional photographer.

Bridal showers are still common but are less traditional. As an alternative, I suggest hosting a relaxing session of beauty at a local day spa. Send out creative invitations to all the guests you would invite to a shower. A rice-paper-lined box filled with bath salts, bath gel, scented soap, lotion, and a small aromatherapy candle is a clever way to let your guests know what they're in for. Remember, for a small group you can easily have the salon come to you or to a beautiful suite at a hotel. This provides a more intimate and private setting for you and your friends.

ANOTHER BRIDE, ANOTHER GROOM, ANOTHER SUNNY HONEYMOON

As you plan your wedding, don't forget the importance of organizing and planning your honeymoon. These plans take time, too. Keep a separate notebook for all your honeymoon plans. Begin making arrangements at least six months before your selected date. Speak to several different travel agents for ideas. Sometimes a travel agent can guide you in a direction you haven't thought of, and your honeymoon will be as special as your wedding day.

9 | Formal Celebrations

"Celebration" is one of my favorite words, and it's one with dozens of wonderful variations: festival, commemoration, revelry, jubilation, carnival. For me, celebration is a way of life. If you really think about it, every day deserves a party—you don't need a reason to do something special.

The most rewarding aspect of my job is participating in the joy that a real celebration holds. I cannot possibly translate into words the emotion of witnessing such bliss fifty-two weeks a year. A husband's genuine shock when he walks into his surprise birthday party . . . and the smile his wife can't hide at pulling it off. The tears of happiness when several generations gather to toast one another and express appreciation for their lives as a family. The look on a bride's face as she enters her wedding ceremony. Sometimes I have to pinch myself and ask, "Do I get paid for this?" I really am the luckiest guy in the world.

Many of my clients say, "Someday I'm just going to throw a party for no reason at all." But for many of us, "someday" never materializes because the stress and emotional strain of playing host overshadows the delight. These concerns often multiply when staging a formal event—without a clear and precise game plan, a formal dinner can be terribly daunting. Certainly the expectations for formal affairs are high—service should be precise and presentation

ABOVE *A gathering of flowers that pick up the colors of the glassware and china helps add a soft touch to this sleek contemporary celebration.*

OPPOSITE *Calla lilies placed blossom-side down in pale blue water provide an easy and chic accent to any contemporary event.*

should be elegant. But a formal party or dinner should never be stuffy; providing a wonderful evening for your guests is still the greatest goal. Remember, no matter how formal an event is, it's still a celebration.

While there are traditional guidelines for formal dining, I have found that for the most part my clients want to incorporate some of those elements but not all of them. A formal dinner party might mean that it is an occasion to get dressed up and have a fancy dinner that is semi-formal in presentation. Unlike other types of par-ties, the elements involved are extremely limited; mostly it's the combination of guests and atmosphere that makes it a truly elegant affair. Formal dinner parties usually take place in the home of the host and/or hostess and have a professional wait staff. They become a rare opportunity for the host to step out of the con-fines of his or her usual entertaining routine. This is the time to break out the good china, fine crystal, and items usually reserved for show.

Any occasion can be the perfect reason to plan a formal dinner. Meeting the new in-laws for the first time, entertaining your boss, a housewarming, a going-away party, a fund-raiser, a special birthday or anniversary celebration are just a few occasions to host a formal dinner. One of my favorite reasons is to gather together with loved ones and celebrate for absolutely no rea-son at all. I think it's fun to get dressed up and use the good china. There's something about putting on a tuxedo at home that makes me feel like royalty, and who doesn't want to feel special in his or her own home?

What separates a formal dinner party from all the rest? The expectations are much greater in terms of detail, service, presentation,

The modern formal dinner party uses a minimalist approach with an artistic style. Here, a runner of rectangular glass vases is filled with colored water and floating candles, which accent the milk glass plates and hand-blown glasses.

A Passion for Parties

A linen runner adds warmth and texture to a sophisticated contemporary metal table.

and formality. What the guests wear, when they arrive, how they are greeted, the length of the cocktail reception, the assigned seating for dinner, and the post-meal repartee are all factored into the formal formula for success. Depending on the occasion, the degree of formality will vary. Official formal dinners, like those hosted at the White House, are the most formal type of parties, and protocol is strictly followed. But for most people there probably aren't many occasions where such conformity is required. That's good news because it allows for more creativity and flexibility in the planning and execution of your own formal dinner. Simple, elegant evenings at home with meals served by the host are still considered formal, especially in this less formal new millennium. There are some general guidelines I suggest to my clients, whether they are planning a state dinner or a bon voyage meal for Mom and Dad. Every successful dinner party, formal or informal, consists of the same five ingredients: a great plan, the right mix of guests, an appropriate and tasty food selection, an elegant table setting, and a gracious host and/or hostess. It's less important to have all matching place settings than it is to create a comfortable setting.

ELEMENTS OF
FORMAL ENTERTAINING

Formal dinner parties do command a certain level of formality, thus the title. That being said, there is a basic procedure to follow when hosting a formal event. From the moment guests arrive, they are greeted by a housekeeper or temporary party help and escorted into a designated cocktail reception area. The host's number one priority is to mingle with guests and greet new arrivals. A formal gathering is an invitation for you as the host to enjoy the entertaining process as much as your guests do. Hiring enough help to accommodate this procedure is a key element to a successful evening.

A formal dinner usually starts off with a set cocktail hour. Guests are then invited to be seated at predetermined assigned chairs. Place cards are always used at formal dinners, especially at larger dinners where a host cannot personally direct the seating. If place cards aren't being used, you need to direct where you'd like everyone seated. Plan ahead so you are gracious and secure about your choices.

SEATING

Formal dinners require a little extra thought than less formal gatherings, especially when it comes to seating. There is nothing worse for a guest than being seated next to someone at a dinner party with whom you have absolutely nothing in common or who is not a conversationalist. Mixing up your guests is important when planning the seating. I try to encourage my clients to split up couples and seat people who don't know each other next to one another. This encourages new and interesting dialogue. If possible, each guest should sit next to someone they know and someone they are meeting for the first time. Honored guests should always be seated next to the host or hostess, preferably to his or her right. There are many choices when planning the seating, so it's important to consider carefully each and every guest's comfort level when making your decisions.

TUTERA TIP: It is traditional for a host to be the last person seated. Remain standing until all your guests have taken their places at the table. Women should always be seated before men, and men should hold the chair for the woman on their right.

SERVICE

A professional staff always serves formal dinner parties. The number of staff needed varies depending on the size of the party. Gatherings of eight to ten guests can easily be accommodated with one or two servers. Larger gatherings require additional servers. Whether you are hosting a small or large dinner, the style of service is exactly the same. A dinner party is all about intimacy and creativity. Running in and out of the kitchen or constantly getting up to change plates for each course is a host's worst nightmare, especially when entertaining formally. Your guests will be more comfortable if you stay seated with them and allow the staff to do the serving.

The staff is generally in black tie, and white-glove service is preferred. Serving dishes are never placed on the table. The staff serves side dishes and bread to guests. Family-style service can be fun but is absolutely inappropriate for a formal dinner party. Every course is prepared in advance and is served on individual plates to each guest. The woman seated nearest to the right of the host is always served first, and the staff continues to serve the guests counterclockwise, serving the hostess and host last.

Six courses are traditional and usually the maximum for formal dinner parties. There is usually a soup or appetizer course to start, followed by a fish course. The entrée is served next, and a salad course follows immediately. Dessert is then served, followed by coffee and after-dinner drinks.

PLACE SETTINGS

A formal table requires that utensils, the centerpiece, and the plates be balanced. Place cards and sometimes menu cards are used when setting a formal table. Generally, a formal place setting consists of the following:

- Service plate
- Butter plate
- Wineglasses, for both red and white wine
- Water glass
- Salad fork, meat fork, and/or fish fork

- Salad knife, meat knife, fish knife, and butter knife

- Soup spoon and/or fruit spoon

- Oyster or seafood fork, if shellfish is being served

- Salt and pepper shakers for every two place settings

- Linen or cloth napkin

Utensils are always set so that the order of use is the same as the order of service, starting from the outside and working toward the service plate. Dessert spoons and forks are served on the dessert plate just before dessert is served. For formal settings, napkins are always placed in the center of the service plate, or are placed to the left of the plate if the first course is in place before guests are seated.

Though most clients prefer traditional place settings for formal dinners, I love to encourage an eclectic mix of crystal, china, and silver whenever possible to make a formal dinner more personalized. It is not necessary that all place settings match. Crystal can be mixed as long as the number of glasses set matches the number of glasses to be used during the meal. I usually try to stay with the tradition of setting the glasses according to size, from largest to smallest. One of my favorite stylistic choices for china is to mix and match colors and patterns. I'll usually stay with one solid service plate, but I might choose to use dinner plates that do not match at all. The butter plates and salad plates can be from an entirely different collection but should be similar in pattern or color to give a planned appearance. The size of the china reflects the importance of each course. The entrée is always served on the largest plate, and the first course, second course, and dessert course are always secondary in size.

TUTERA TIP: A fingernail away from the edge of the table is the best way to measure the placement of all silverware and the bottom of the base plate. This helps keep a perfect placement of all table settings. Also, make sure no flatware is under the rim of the plate.

For the most elegant events, select colors and dinner wares for your tables that coordinate with the room.

THE EVENT: A Formal Valentine's Day Birthday Celebration

THE SETTING The formal dining room of my client's mansion in Bel Air, California. This room had been re-created with the look and style of Versailles; therefore, only the most elegantly planned evening would work in this environment. Opulence was the key!

NUMBER OF GUESTS Twenty-two of my client's dearest friends.

THE PLACE SETTING All of my client's fine crystal, china, and silverware were used for this occasion. Fortunately, she has the best quality. Selecting from the various patterns and styles was somewhat difficult because there were so many to choose from. Placement of her china and crystal was extremely important to her. Each glass was perfectly placed so that each side of the table was mirrored in it. Formal place cards were carefully positioned around a long dining table that was set for the twenty-two guests. An unusual duplicate place setting for the hostess was put at both ends of the table to allow her to move and socialize with the guests at either end of the table. This wonderful and unexpected personal touch allows the host or hostess to be especially social throughout the dinner.

THE TABLE RUNNER DESIGN A runner of low flowers in deep dramatic colors ran the entire length of the table. The flowers were in bright yellow, deep purple, hot pinks, golden oranges, and striking reds. This festive floral runner was designed via color blocking, which allowed the colors of the flowers to be clustered in specific color tones and then bleed from one color to the next. This allowed primary colors to appear formal and sophisticated rather than informal and casual. As each color melted into the next, it had an embellishment of whole and sliced fruits that perfectly matched the flower color. Lemons were placed with the yellow flowers, tangerines were placed with the orange flowers, and so forth.

Crystal roping from the chandeliers was added for an even more glamorous finish to the lighting fixtures that already existed. The

Symmetry is a key element to setting a formal table.

TUTERA TIP: To provide additional space for a formal dinner, replace your dining room chairs with smaller ballroom chairs from a local party supply rental company.

ABOVE *A column gave height to a large floral design and created another focus within the room.*

OPPOSITE *A small cluster of roses provided a perfect accent to each place setting.*

crystal roping was woven throughout the entire runner and spilled onto the table, adding an extra sparkle to the table and a refined finish. Two magnificent eighteenth-century candelabras were placed in the center of the table, adding extra height to the centerpiece. The candles used on the table matched the colors of the candles in the main centerpiece. Table linens were custom-made in shades of rich purple and lavender on dupionni silk and bengaline; these colors were hand-picked to match the draperies hanging in the dining room. Custom-made cushions for the ballroom chairs completed the look for this very personalized formal dinner.

THE NAPKIN TREATMENT This was a Valentine's birthday celebration, so each napkin was tied with a beautiful cluster of either pink or red spray roses. Keeping with the design of the formal look, they were tied with antique gold–colored cording and tassels that matched those on the window draperies.

THE MENU My client and her personal chef carefully selected the five courses to be served, each on its own set of china, that had five very different looks. Wines complemented each course. The courses were presented on a stunning charger plate. The china was very simple and understated so as not to take away from the presentation of the magnificent food.

THE PLACE CARDS AND MENU CARDS Custom-printed menu cards and place cards were provided, as they should be for any formal sit-down dinner at home. A card listing the wines to be served for each course was also displayed.

THE SERVICE Butlers were positioned around the perimeter of the dining room at all times. I suggest one butler per three guests if possible. For this party I provided one main butler to service the hostess throughout the entire evening, to make sure every detail was perfect. A butler is always used for service, and the clean-up staff is to sweep the table, making sure all finished or dirty plates are quickly removed.

THE EVENT: A Formal Housewarming Celebration

THE SETTING My client's formal dining room in Westchester, New York.

NUMBER OF GUESTS Eight friends.

THE FLOWERS The entire dining room table was a carpet of flowers: roses, hydrangea petals, freesia, and orchids. The flowers spilled off one side and onto the floor into a stunning puddle, adding to this award-winning fantasy floral design. The design began with color blocking, using regular foam board to set up the layout. By using this pre-layout, we were able to minimize waste by ordering the precise number of flowers needed. We used the color-blocking technique to section off the floral design within this "blanket." By color blocking the floral, we were able to create a continuous flow that gave the flowers the appearance of melting together.

Create a garden table using moss and flowers to cover the tabletop.

THE PLACE SETTING Wedgewood china, Waterford crystal, and Christofle flatware were placed on individual slate place mats. Each mat was finished with a border of moss, adding to the feeling of an outdoor garden setting. A sweep of cascading flowers attached to each napkin added detail and texture to the place setting.

TUTERA TIP: Never take things too seriously. An aura of something unexpected should be incorporated in all parties. It allows guests to wonder about what might be around the corner, creating an anticipation of surprise.

This spectacular napkin treatment used a mix of flower heads woven together with fine wire.

THE MENU Because the setting was so opulent and over the top, my client and I decided to keep the food simple. In keeping with the style and flavor of this elegant formal dinner party, all the courses were served with the expectation of a formal affair, but the menu had a whimsical twist. Cream cheese and jelly sandwiches garnished with a small touch of caviar were served as the first course. The second course was a colorful tropical fruit and greens salad, adding texture and color to each place setting. The entrée was a delicious gourmet turkey burger served with grilled vegetables and a puff pasty filled with mushrooms. French-style sweet potato fries were also offered to each guest.

A MODERN LOOK FOR A
FORMAL DINNER PARTY

A formal dinner party doesn't have to appear ornate and stuffy. I designed a formal table for the annual fund-raiser given by the Design Industries Foundation Fighting AIDS. Although the table shown here is formal in appearance, the style and design are clearly forward thinking and modern. The table was a custom-designed brushed stainless steel rectangle with matching chairs. A long white box filled with water served as a runner down the length of the table. Glass crystals were placed inside the runner to reflect the chandeliers overhead. Everything on the table, from the rectangular box of candles to the flower arrangements, stemmed from the runner. The centerpieces were stainless-steel bowls filled with limes, lemons, and oranges. Additionally, four stainless-steel candle stands were placed evenly across the table and were filled with roses that matched the lemons, limes, and oranges, as well as orchids, exotic lilies, and tulips. A snakelike arrangement of pink, yellow, and orange roses zigzagged under the box runner, giving the impression of a giant flower boa.

     The lampshades covering the chandeliers were covered with daisies that matched the citrus fruits, giving an even more whimsical look to the table design. Each place setting had a frosted charger plate with silver beads around the perimeter, tying in the look of the stainless steel. Each course was served on smaller frosted plates. An individual silver caviar bowl was placed at each setting. Green Granny Smith apples sat in the bowls for added color, and they were later removed and replaced with luscious black caviar.

     The stemware was made from colorful lime green blown glass. The napkins were placed in hammered napkin rings made of silver. The overall look was funky and industrial, yet with a level of elegance. This was a perfect example of creating an individual look for an affair, formal or informal.

To change the look of any chandelier and give it a whimsical air, glue daisy heads to inexpensive lampshades.

THE EVENT: The Swan House Ball

THE SETTING The grounds of Atlanta's famous 1920s Historical Society Home, known as the Swan House.

THE HOST The Swan House is one of Atlanta's most treasured post–Civil War homes, and an invitation to the annual ball is the most coveted of the year in Atlanta. The purpose of the event is to raise funds to preserve the Swan House and to promote education at the historical center. The committee had contacted me after reading about other events I had planned in Greater Atlanta, including a birthday party given by performer Elton John, a sometimes Atlanta resident.

Swags of sheer white fabric were draped from the ceiling to add intimacy to a huge tent.

THE CONCEPT The chairwoman of the event explained to me that this annual fete had always been planned around some elaborate theme, but it was her desire to do something different. I thought we might return to Atlanta's richly rooted history and plan an elegant evening of southern warmth and hospitality. After rejecting my original idea to burn the Swan House down and rebuild a replica of Tara on the property, I was pretty sure the committee wasn't taking me very seriously when I walked them through my ideas.

I surveyed the entire area for swans—not a one in sight. Okay, I really surveyed the grounds for tenting ideas and then the interior of the historic home. It was then that I decided to have the guests feel as though they were enjoying an intimate meal within the home regardless of where they were seated, indoors or outdoors. Fortunately, the event committee agreed. And in case you're wondering, I didn't really propose burning

A replica of the Swan House's crest was reproduced on what is usually a plain dance floor.

down the house. I'm saving that idea for the premiere party when they remake the 1970s blockbuster *Towering Inferno.*

The outdoor tent was divided into three spaces to give the feeling of three separate rooms. An abundance of flowers played an enormous role in the look of the rooms and created a truly opulent setting.

Guests entered into a magical European courtyard after descending a stone staircase, which I adorned in garlands of flowers. Customized chiffon draperies hung throughout all three rooms, giving them an elegant flowy mood. Each panel was illuminated by nine crystal chandeliers. The drapery panels helped create settings that allowed each table's guests to sense the intimacy of the evening. I didn't want any table to feel more or less important than another, and the close proximity of each room accomplished this task. I also had a hand-painted terrazzo dance floor built; it was 32 by 32 feet and had the Swan House's logo incorporated into the design.

THE FLOWERS This party took place in Atlanta in early May, when it can be very hot and humid. I needed to use flowers that could withstand the heat and humidity without drooping or wilting before the guests arrived. I chose French tulips, calla lilies, peonies, flowering branches, roses, and viburnum, which can be fragile, but the party was enclosed and took place in an air-conditioned environment. Every table had a slightly different look for its centerpiece, with colors of yellow, orange, red, hot pink, and celadon green. Some centerpieces were tall arrangements flowing out of crystal and silver containers, while others were low arrangements. Every centerpiece contained a candlelit lamp covered with either a fabric or a beaded shade. Crystal and silver candleholders were on either side of the centerpiece. When lit, the low light was romantic and flattering.

THE TABLE SETTINGS All the flowers used were very vibrant in color. For balance I chose to keep the table settings and linens rather simple in color and design. The chairs were covered in chiffon to match the ceiling treatments. The tablecloths were a monochromatic celadon green. The cloth had a fleur-de-lis pattern, and the overlay was sheer chiffon with a satin border. The solid cream cloth napkins were held together by a nosegay of flowers that matched each centerpiece. The table settings were simple silver flatware, basic white china, and crystal stemware, which truly allowed everything else in the table design to stand out.

Using a tall stand like this crystal column to display the flowers on each table adds dramatic impact to this elegantly draped tent. Elevating the flowers allows there to be little obstruction across the table.

I love working in the South, particularly Atlanta. The Swan House ladies were truly appreciative of the design and allowed me to push the creative envelope a little further than in previous events they had hosted. Their trust and faith in my abilities resulted in a beautiful, unforgettable evening and a tremendous fund-raising effort.

I have found that fund-raisers tend to be more lucrative if the guests are dazzled and have a really good time. Whenever I am hired to produce a fund-raising event, my goal is to help the organization surpass their numbers from previous years. I accomplish this by providing themes and details not usually associated with charitable functions. Many times organizations trying to raise funds and/or awareness are afraid to throw a real splashy event because they fear that patrons may view it as a misappropriation of the organization's money. This may occasionally be true, but for the events that I participate in, budget is weighed very heavily against the desired outcome. Together with the committee or chairperson, I am able to formulate the perfect balance and create a very special event for a very special cause, whatever it might be.

10 | Holiday Entertaining

I love celebrating the holidays. Some of my favorite events have been planned around the holiday season from Thanksgiving to New Year's. Although I'm continuously busy throughout the year, there is something about these six weeks that brings me a special joy and pride as a party planner and event producer. The holidays are a time of bringing families together and celebrating old traditions. Of course the holidays are also a time to start new traditions! Over the years I have been privileged to help decorate the home of Vice President and Mrs. Gore for the Christmas season and help plan unforgettable holiday parties for numerous clients.

More than any other time of year, the holiday season seems to offer a reason to throw a real bash, to celebrate. The same principles apply for holiday entertaining as for any other kind of party, but with a unique twist when it comes to decorating and atmosphere. There is one more detail to consider when hosting a holiday party: how to survive! As with any party you plan or host, having a well-thought-out strategy and keeping your sense of humor will help see you through this very special time.

I chose three of my favorite events of recent years to highlight how special the holidays can be. And there is also one for those of you who love the summer.

A combination of flowering paperwhites, seasonal garlands, and richly decorated candelabras made a beautiful design along the center of this holiday dining room table.

171

THE EVENT: Thanksgiving in the City

THE SETTING An apartment in New York City on Park Avenue overlooking Central Park.

THE DESIGN The hostess wanted to have a casual and symbolic setting for her family's annual Thanksgiving celebration that utilized her very formal dining table. The environment in the apartment was formal, but my clients were rather down-to-earth, so I thought I'd balance the look of the home with the personalities of the host and hostess. I decided to make the design rustic, but keep it simply beautiful.

THE TABLE DESIGN First, I covered the table with foam board, available at any art supply store. This allowed me to set anything I liked on the top without damaging the table. The foam board is placed over table pads to ensure safety for the table. I covered the foam board surface with terra-cotta-colored tumbled marble, which had an earthy look that played into the fall foliage because of the orange and rust colors. To fill in the spaces, I rubbed the entire table with moss, which filled the crevices between the tiles. This gave a feeling of the earth, symbolic of the harvest associated with Thanksgiving.

Large birch tree logs (that would later be used for firewood) were set as the "anchor" for the runner. Placed among the logs was a variety of crystal bowls and canisters that held cranberries, some of which fell onto the tabletop. Beautiful flowers and other fruit representing the holiday were also placed in the bowls and canisters. Hollowed-out gourds and small pumpkins served as vases for the flowers. This really added

Natural landscape elements (right) created a more casual Thanksgiving centerpiece while remaining true to the theme of American bounty. Copper placemats along with the hostess's own coordinating china were set on stone tiles to create an elegant yet untraditional Thanksgiving tableau.

TUTERA TIP: Use unusual and creative containers such as small pumpkins or other dense vegetables to hold flower arrangements during the holidays. It is an inexpensive and disposable way to create a custom look. It also makes a lovely gift for guests to take home.

Combining birch logs, flowers, and gourds created a rustic setting.

a natural beauty designed to bring the guests into nature, while dining on Park Avenue!

Large, chunky, round candles lined with cinnamon sticks (purchased from Pottery Barn) were set on small antique stands and placed directly on the table. To add an interesting twist, the table was set with a mixture of the hostess's fine china, crystal, and flatware. I loved that the guests ate off expensive place settings mixed with inexpensive decorations. The combination was rustic elegance—perfect for Thanksgiving in the City.

THE MENU Louis Lanza, chef and owner of Josie's and Citrus Bar and Grill in New York City, provided the delicious catering for this fantastic Thanksgiving celebration.

AN ALMOST TRADITIONAL THANKSGIVING

Serves 12

Roasted Butternut Squash Soup

12-Grain Biscuits with Horseradish-Infused Butter

20-pound Roasted Free-Range Pasilla Chile and Cinnamon-Rubbed Turkey

Giblet Gravy

Corn Bread, Pecan, and Fresh Cranberry Dressing

Cranberry-Ginger-Pear Chutney

Baked Apples with Raisins and Cinnamon

Zucchini Pancakes

Oven Parsnips and Carrots with Rosemary

Slow-Cooked String Beans with Smoked Chicken Sausage

Fruit Pie with Macadamia Crusted Top

Pumpkin Carrot Cake

THE EVENT: Christmas in Connecticut

THE LOCATION The historical home of clients in Connecticut that was built in 1891.

THE SETTING A fairy-tale mansion in the woods.

THE DESIGN This particular client owns a chain of boutique-style gift stores and coffee shops, so during the holiday season she is too busy to decorate her home. She approached me with the project of preparing her family's holiday decorations, and I was elated. Her home is my dream house, and if she ever put it on the market, I'd snatch it up in a second. I was able to hand-pick all the decorations I wanted from her amazing shops, and I felt like a kid in a candy store.

THE LIGHTING Holiday lighting is very important, especially when decorating a home of this size and grandeur. I wanted passersby to gaze in awe at the home's expression of the season. I hired a lighting company to install lights on the outside of this magnificent home. I up-lit the house in alternating red and green lights, washing the entire front in those holiday hues. Miniature juniper trees on the front porch were covered in small white lights. This provided an intimate touch in front of such a large home. Tiny white lights ran along the entire edge of the back porch, like delicate icicles hanging from the arches. This tactic allowed my client to enjoy the lighting from inside her home.

THE TREES Three Christmas trees were placed inside the home. The first, a traditional tree in the family room, had classic-looking ornaments, multicolored lights, and the added touch of real candy canes. The next tree, of sheer elegance, was set in the alcove of the amazing formal living room. It was covered in tiny white lights and delicate ornaments. Hand-tied bows of silk shantung in solid mango, hot pink, and gold and plaid made the tree seemed dressed for the occasion. The colors complemented the wall treatments of the room. The outcome was the "picture-perfect tree." The third tree was set up in the kids' playroom. While I had been able to decorate the trees in the main areas of the home as I deemed best, I wanted my client's children to experience

For a striking and unified look, use the same ribbons on your packages and to decorate your tree.

TUTERA TIP: Floodlights can be purchased from Home Depot or a similar store and red and green bulbs can be placed in the sockets to create a Christmas effect at your home. *Caution:* Make sure all electrical wires are grounded for outdoor use.

the thrill of decorating their own tree for Christmas. I helped with the lights on the tree, but the kids did the rest themselves. Handmade ornaments from school, past and present, and their favorites covered the tree from top to bottom. The key was to let the children's imaginations go wild and let them enjoy the season.

OTHER HOLIDAY DECORATIONS This fantastic home has twelve fireplaces. I thought it would be fun to create a decor for each one around *my* version of the "Twelve Days of Christmas." I decorated each fireplace mantel with a specific theme based on the twelve themes that were reminiscent of the season. The fireplace in the formal dining room was all white and had an antique mirror hanging above it. The feeling was very clean and pure, like snow, so I placed fifteen different snowmen, in different sizes and styles, on a bed of Christmas tree branches and greens, adding contrast to all the white. I draped strings of crystals (available at any home improvement store or lighting company) along the edge of the fireplace and mantel. These crystals are an inexpensive way to add sparkle and formality to any setting. Between the swags of crystals I hung simple yet elegant round glass ornaments. Each ornament hung at a different level and was tied with a see-through iridescent opaque ribbon.

Ornaments mixed with ribbons and garlands are a simple way to dress up a mantel over the holidays.

In the living room, since the tree was elegant and formal, I decorated the fireplace a little less formally. It was covered with a variety of carved wood animals. A garland and the same silk ribbon that was used on the tree coordinated the overall feel of the room. The fireplace in the study was simple and masculine. A variety of antique nutcrackers imported from Germany were set among a small amount of Christmas greens placed atop the mantel. The edge was accented with miniature nutcrackers hanging like fringe. For the fireplace in the family room, which was traditional like the tree that stood beside it, I draped garland and a wide plaid

Christmas ribbon, and topped the mantel with antique angels. The theme was representative of peace for the season. The next fireplace was decorated for the children's enjoyment with a variety of teddy bears dressed for Christmas sitting on top of fresh Christmas greens.

One of the most beautiful and amazing fireplaces was in the main entrance of the home. Since Santa Claus is one of the most visible symbols of the holiday, this mantel featured a variety of Santas. Garland was also draped along the sides of the mantel and accented with tiny white lights that led to a huge Santa holding a bag of gifts. I placed a plate of cookies on the mantel to represent the traditional offering families leave for the big guy. As a finishing touch, the entire banister in the foyer was covered in a garland of festive holiday ribbon.

TUTERA TIP: Providing a separate dining table for the younger kids is a great way to keep them entertained, calm, and still part of the holiday. The kids' table should be shorter in height than a regular table, and you can rent kid-size chairs. They will feel more important and have a lot more fun. Place a fully decorated miniature Christmas tree in the center of the table for a whimsical touch.

THE EVENT: A New Year's Eve Celebration

THE LOCATION The newly finished log cabin home of my clients in Westchester County, New York.

THE SETTING The wooded backyard of the family estate.

THE CONCEPT This was the only party I planned for the turn of the century. Though I was asked to plan major extravaganzas from Atlantic City to New York City, I chose to plan only one event for this important milestone. My clients were the family of other clients I have worked closely with over the years, and I wanted to help plan this dreamlike spectacle to ring in the new year and new century. The evening was a perfect finale to six months of planning and preparation. This party, like the turn of the century, was a once-in-a-lifetime event for everyone involved.

The evening began with cocktails inside the clients' new home. Guests were greeted with a glass of champagne in the front courtyard and then guided to a wide-open space on the first level of the home. The house was positioned in such a way that guests had no idea there was an enormous tent erected at the back of the home. Since the house was an elaborate log cabin, I decided to play on the juxtaposition of the home. The cocktail space was designed to match the log cabin feel while the main party space was characterized by sleek decor, lively entertainment, and exotic food. The back of the home had continuous French doors, and these were kept closed until the end of the cocktail hour. Jazz played over the house system during cocktails and flowed into the tent when it was time for the guests to move inside. At just the right moment the doors were opened and the tented space was grandly unveiled. As they did, the music became livelier, so everyone knew where to go.

The tent was extremely sturdy, and guests felt as if they were still inside a permanent structure. It took three weeks to install the tent. The walls and ceiling were draped with white chiffon fabric, pleated and pulled to perfection. White carpet covered the floor except for the glossy white space in the center for dancing. This was not a sit-down dinner, so I carefully created areas within the large tent

Dining tables (top) were stylishly mixed between standard square tables covered with slate and high brushed-metal tables with white bar stools. Offerings at the buffet stations (bottom) were indicated humorously: A wall of glass bowls filled with eggs signaled the omelet station, and hundreds of goldfish pointed out the seafood station.

TUTERA TIP: Be sure there
is plenty of space around
the buffet area to allow easy
movement.

for guests to eat. The furniture, including sofas, cocktail tables, bar stools, lamps, and wall sconces, created an intimate setting.

An enormous three-tier crystal chandelier was hung at the entrance of the tent to create an impression of grandeur. Below it was a round table with a beautiful centerpiece made from simple wheat grass, green apples, and small silver-encased candles. A long table was set on either side, and a row of three smaller crystal chandeliers hung above each one. This setup allowed those who wanted to sit while eating to do so. This is important when having a variety of age groups at a party without a structured sit-down dinner. Older guests may not be comfortable standing to eat. Remember, you want everyone to be as comfortable as possible, and this includes your curiously good-looking distant cousin who never seems to show up with a date, yet ends up shirtless and leading a conga line with the waiters by the end of the evening.

Identical buffet stations were placed in the rear corners of the tent, and two bars were in the front corners. In addition, I designed two unique stations on opposite sides of the tent. To the left was a sushi bar and to the right a vodka and caviar bar. Those who just wanted to nibble instead of eating an entire plateful of food were able to do so. The sushi bar was made from four large fish tanks topped with a thick plate of Plexiglas. The tanks were filled with a variety of goldfish, which were given as favors at the end of the evening in small crystal fish bowls with the client's name and the date of celebration: 1-1-2000! The caviar and vodka bar was as simple and elegant as the offerings: a long wooden bar covered in white padded fabric, a thick piece of white marble on top, beautiful candles, and silver pedestals to hold the caviar and accoutrements.

For additional seating, two "lounges" were created in the corners of the sunken dance floor, which was in the center of the tent. Identical white sectionals were placed on a bed of grass—so that the guests would feel as if they were at both a chic club and a theater space. The tiered approach gave the sensation of being in a Broadway theater: the dance floor was the lowest level; the guest and buffet tables surrounding it were on the next level; and the multilevel stage was the highest tier.

THE ENTERTAINMENT A stage was built behind the dance floor for the entertainers. A DJ was placed fourteen feet above the guests' heads, giving the illusion of a nightclub. His oversize white leather chair served as a perfect base for him to spin.

This was a night like no other, so only one entertainer would not suffice. I created a night of disco divas. First, Alicia Bridges performed her famous single "I Love the Nightlife." Then the group Musique played a forty-five-minute set, including their hit song "Push Push in the Bush." Finally, Lisa Lisa of Cult Jam fame brought the house down with her music and fabulous dancers.

Having three different entertainers along with a DJ allowed the guests to hear something they liked and have a great time. The evening was a continuous build of entertainment suspense and surprises, the perfect schedule for such a magical millennium evening. Four sexy go-go dancers dressed in silver outfits danced on clear Plexiglas boxes, which were dramatically up-lit from inside, adding to this theatrical night.

THE MENU Hors d'oeuvres were served during cocktails. Small, unique food was served, both hot and cold, but everything was bite size. (You don't want to serve anything too messy or too big, especially at a black-tie event.) The waiters were instructed to keep a continuous flow of food but not to offer the same item simultaneously. The buffet stations offered a variety of grilled fish, vegetables, and crepes. The sushi bar had a variety "made to order." After the midnight countdown, a dessert buffet that replaced the dinner stations enticed the guests with a variety of sweets, coffee and tea choices, and cordials. At 2:00 A.M., we opened a breakfast bar, complete with made-to-order omelets and a bagel-and-lox spread that would be the envy of your favorite deli. This was a welcome surprise to guests who had worked up a hearty appetite dancing and ringing in the new year.

TUTERA TIP: When your party isn't a sit-down affair, make sure there is adequate seating for your guests. It is also a good idea to make provisions for sufficient bathroom facilities.

By giving each table its own identity, we were able to create a more intimate dining experience within the context of a much larger party.

THE EVENT: A Memorial Day Clambake

I invited several friends to my home in East Hampton, New York, for a casual dinner to celebrate the beginning of summer, my favorite time of year. I wanted the night to be fun and festive, and the theme was to be a surprise. Clambakes don't always have to be on the beach or in Elvis Presley movies. In fact, even the sand is optional. The only *real* requirement is clams. This was such an easy party to pull together, and it was very cute. And it didn't cost me a bucket of clams, either.

THE LOCATION My house is not particularly nautical in decor, so once I chose the clambake theme, I needed to add a little extra beach atmosphere to my weekend country farm home.

The party was to take place in the backyard. I needed a table long enough to seat eight people comfortably. Since I'm not a conventional guy, a regular picnic table with benches just wouldn't do. I started off at an antique store looking for a farm table. After pricing them, I realized it was more money than I needed to spend. It occurred to me that I could duplicate the look with a door of some kind. But where does one buy a door that looks like an antique?

I went to a local junkyard and looked for a wooden plank door that was clean and level. I found the perfect door: It was white, in excellent condition, and cost only $30. But what was I going to use as a pedestal to support it? I found two battered birdbaths of the same height; as luck would have it, they were standard table height. The birdbaths cost $75. I asked the junkyard attendant to help me cut a hole in the center of the door that would allow me to use an umbrella. I liked the idea of having a doorknob on the door so that the table would become a conversation piece. I searched through bins of knobs and found a spectacular aged all-bronze knob. It was perfect and was only $5. So there I was in all my junkyard glory, having spent only $110 for a masterpiece table. I used an eclectic mix of chairs from my home, and the table looked great even before I set it.

THE TABLE SETTING It's amazing what you can do with ordinary dishtowels and yesterday's newspaper. Knowing that clams can be messy, I didn't want to use any of my matching expensive linens to set the table. I actually loved the idea of not matching anything for

An old door was used as the table, creating an inexpensive, comfortable, and casual setting that can be left outdoors all summer.

When buying seafood, make sure you get the freshest available. Buy it on the day of the party and keep it refrigerated until you are ready to prepare the meal.

once. The assortment of colors adds a lively flair to an otherwise black-and-white newspaper tablecloth. The newspaper cost 50 cents, and each of the dishtowels was less than $2. For an extra touch, I bought eight miniature terra-cotta clay pots, knocked the bottoms off them, and used the remainder of the pot as napkin rings. My everyday china and silverware were the place settings, which worked well because the colors are not consistent. I used clear Mason jars for drinking glasses and served homemade pink lemonade, with the fresh lemons still in the bowl.

THE MENU

Serves 8

3 two-pound lobsters

3 pounds of New England steamers

3 pounds mussels

3 pounds littleneck clams

2 pounds shelled shrimp

2 pounds hot Italian sausage

Onions, leeks, and potatoes stewed in white wine

8 ears of corn

Coleslaw

2 bottles of merlot

2 bottles of chardonnay

THE ATMOSPHERE With all the color already in place, I didn't think I needed an elaborate floral arrangement. Because I live near the water and the woods, mosquitoes can be a real nuisance in the summer months, so citronella candles were a must for the night. I placed the candles in two locations to ensure a no-buzzing zone. One set of candles, placed in large hurricane glass containers, was on the table on a runner of sand, and the other set hung from the opened umbrella. The glow from the hanging candles beautifully illuminated the whole table and served as the only source of light after dusk. One final touch was placing the heads of yellow daisies inside the hurricane glasses, on the napkins, and along the sand runner.

This party was so much fun, and I recently sold the concept to a client who wants to expand the number of guests to 250. She is using her own backyard (mine is way too small) but otherwise is keeping everything pretty much the same. There's just one problem: Where am I going to find a door that seats 250 people?

Acknowledgments

This book has taken me on a wonderful creative journey. Many people have made this project extraordinarily special and rewarding each step of the way, and I'd like to offer them my deepest thanks.

Without the love, support, and positive encouragement that my parents have shown me my entire life, I am certain that my dreams would not have come true. They have provided an unconditional love that I find a remarkable inspiration every day. Mom and Dad, thank you for giving me your best and showing me exactly who I hope to become. Jo Ann, you always offer a mother's love, yet still manage my entire life (not to mention my company) with grace and elegance. My brother, Gregg, and sister, Amy, have always been great supporters as well. I also want to thank my aunt Maria, whose spiritual connection is an added source of strength and inspiration in my life.

I would like to offer many heartfelt thanks, much gratitude, and total love to my partner in life, Ryan Jurica. You are my breath of fresh air, my angel. You always make me feel that nothing is a challenge, but rather just a goal to achieve. My unconditional love to you always.

Joseph and Mary Corsaro, my grandparents, have been an important factor in my success. Grandfather, you have been with me from the very beginning stages of my career, you taught me the flower business, and you have passed along the brilliant knowledge that I use every working day to keep my company alive. Nana, your words of wisdom and advice continue to make me a stronger and better person. And your dignity and graciousness toward others has taught me to treat people how I want to be treated. Thank you also to my Nanny, Josephine Tutera, for always taking an interest in my life and saving every newspaper clipping.

My entire staff has been instrumental in the success of my company and in the creation of this book, and I owe them a great debt of gratitude. This talented crew is able to execute the thousands of ideas that flow through my head every day. A special thanks goes to Shawn Rabideau, my personal assistant; his attention to detail and dedication to this project put me at ease and kept me on schedule. And Diane Wagner's beautiful and creative floral work is a wonderful addition.

The continued support and guidance of Kevyn and Ken de Regt have allowed me to push ahead and succeed, and I cannot thank them enough.

To all of my clients, who have made it possible to build a business I can be proud of, thank you for believing in me, one and all. All have trusted my creativity and allowed me to design and produce events that have made them smile with excitement.

I'd like to thank my agents at the William Morris Agency. Mel Berger, my literary agent, believed in the book and shared my vision. Also, my gratitude to Donna Bagdasarian, Glen Gulino, and Jon Rosen.

A heartfelt thanks is offered to everyone at Simon & Schuster, including my publisher, David Rosenthal, and my incredible and supportive editor, Constance Herndon, who saw the beauty of this book. Stephen Motika has helped keep everything together; Ginger Barton has created the party passion buzz; and Isolde Sauer and Peter McCulloch have smoothed its production.

I am particularly grateful to designer Joel Avirom for helping to bring my aesthetic vision for this book to life. Thanks also to my incredible publicist, Sarah Hall, and her staff, for always knowing exactly what I need and how to make it happen—in a bigger, bolder way than anyone else I know.

The following vendors lent their support and knowledge in the making of this book. They have been a great pleasure to work with and I thank them from the bottom of my heart: MyClementine.com; Jerry Hatch at ABC Carpet and Home; David Castle at Sonnier & Castle Catering; Chris Starr at Starr Tents; Barbara, Steve, and Michael Davis, Frost Lighting; Steve Maronian at Sweet Lisa's Exquisite Cakes; Laura Leigh at Alpine Creative Group; and Frank Lombardi, Frank Paleo, Wendy Rabb, Sidni Greenblatt, Linda Gardner, Sue Katz, Terri Bergman, and Ruth Fischl.

Andre Baranowski's photographs continue to make my work look wonderful. Thank you for being patient and providing your talents. Thanks, also, to each of the following photographers for making my work look great: Nadine Froger, Jean-Jacques Pochet, Michael Kress, Tom Rollo, Ron Aira, and Judy Lawne.

I also have the deepest gratitude to express to my dear friend Laura Morton, without whom this book would not have happened. Laura, having you as a friend is special, but to have you as a coauthor is incredible. Thank you for teaching me along the way. We had so much fun and you touched me more deeply than you will know.

Index